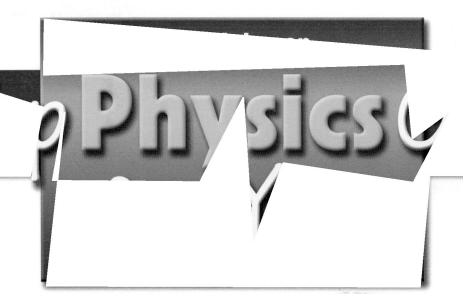

Physics

Contents

Introduction

Revision Technique

Examination Technique

Revision Calendar (detachable, for your bedroom wall)

Revision Cards (detachable, for revision in spare moments)

To see the latest Exam Specification for AQA Modular Science, visit **www.aqa.org.uk**

To see this Exam Specification 'mapped' with the relevant pages in *Physics for You*,
visit **www.physicsforyou.co.uk**

Introduction

Top Physics Grades for You is designed to help you achieve the best possible grades in your GCSE examination.

It focuses on exactly what you need to do to succeed in the AQA Modular Science exam (for Single or for Double Award, and at either Foundation or Higher Tier), or in the AQA Modular Physics exam.

There is a separate book for AQA Coordinated Science and AQA Physics B.

This revision book is best used together with the ***Physics for You*** textbook, but it can also be used by itself.

There are also books for
Top Biology Grades for You and
Top Chemistry Grades for You.

For each section in the AQA Modular Science examination specification, there is a Topic as shown on the opposite page.

For each Topic there are 2 double-page spreads:
- a **Revision** spread, which shows you exactly what you need to know (see below), and
- a **Questions** spread, which lets you try out some exam questions on this topic.
  The **Answers** for these, with Examiner's Tips, are given at the back of the book.

In addition, for each section of Topics there is:
- a **Sample Answer** spread, showing you answers at Grade-A level and at Grade-C level, with Examiner's Comments and Tips. These will help you to focus on how to improve, to move up to a higher grade.

Each Revision spread is laid out clearly, using boxes:

Each spread starts with some 'ThinkAbout' questions, to help you focus on the topic. The answers are shown at the bottom of the page.

Topic number.

The pages show essential content for the exam.

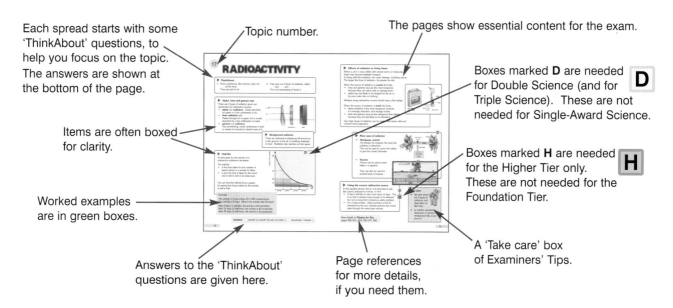

Boxes marked **D** are needed for Double Science (and for Triple Science). These are not needed for Single-Award Science.

Boxes marked **H** are needed for the Higher Tier only. These are not needed for the Foundation Tier.

Items are often boxed for clarity.

Worked examples are in green boxes.

Answers to the 'ThinkAbout' questions are given here.

Page references for more details, if you need them.

A 'Take care' box of Examiners' Tips.

As a first step, go through this book and:
- If you are studying for Single-Award Science, cross out all the boxes labelled **D**
- If you are studying for the Foundation Tier, cross out all the boxes labelled **H**
- If you are **not** studying for Triple Award Physics, cross out all of Topics 21, 22, 23.

Then use the pull-out **Revision Calendar** to keep a record of your progress.

At the back of the book there are detachable **Revision Cards**, with very brief summaries.

You can use these to top up your revision in spare moments – for example, when sitting on a bus or waiting for a lesson.

Best wishes for a great result in your exams.

Keith Johnson

Revision Technique

Prepare

1. Go through the book, crossing out any boxes that you don't need (as described at the bottom of page 3).

2. While doing this, you can decide which are your strong topics, and which are topics that you need to spend more time on.

3. You need to balance your time between:
   - **Revising** what you need to know about Physics.
     To do this, use the first double-page spread in each topic.
   - **Practising** by doing exam questions.
     To do this, use the second spread in each topic.
   Do these two things for each topic in turn.

Revise

4. Think about your best ways of revising. Some of the best ways are to do something *active*. To use active learning you can:
   - Write down **notes**, as a summary of the topic (while reading through the double-page spread).
     Use highlighter pens to colour key words.
   - Make a **poster** to summarise each topic (and perhaps pin it up on your bedroom wall).
     Make it colourful, and use images/sketches if you can.
   - Make a spider-diagram or **mind map** of each topic.
     See the example here, but use your own style:
   - Ask someone (family or friend) to **test** you on the topic.
   - **Teach** the topic to someone (family or friend).
   Which method works best for you?

5. It is usually best to work in a quiet room, for about 25–30 minutes at a time, and then take a 5–10 minute break.

6. After you have revised a topic, make a note of the date on the pull-out **Revision Calendar**.

Practise

7. When you have revised a topic, and think you know it well, then it's important to practise it, by answering some **exam questions**. Turn to the second spread of the topic and answer the questions as well as you can.

8. When you have finished them, turn to the **Examination answers and tips** that start on page 108.
   Check your answers, and read the Examiner's Tips.
   Can you see how to improve your answers in future?

9. Keep a record of your progress on the **Revision Calendar**.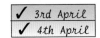

Re-revise and Top-up

10. It is important to re-revise each topic again, after an interval.
    The best intervals are after 10 minutes, after 1 day, and after 1 week (see the graphs in *Physics for You*, pages 382–383).

    For this top-up you can use the topic spread, your notes, poster or mindmap, and the **Revision Cards** at the back of this book.

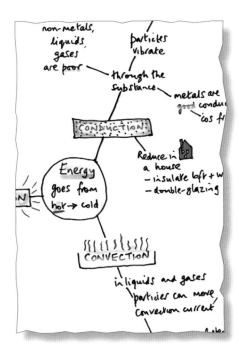

*Part of a **Mind Map** for Topic 1 : Conduction, Convection, Radiation.*

*A Mind Map always makes more sense when you make it **yourself**.*

Use colour and images if you can.

A revision flowchart:

Choose a topic to revise.

1. Revise

- **ThinkAbout** : try the questions in the ThinkAbout box.
  The answers are at the bottom of the page.

- **Read** the rest of the double-page spread.
  Focus on any parts you are not sure about.

- **Do** make Notes, or a Poster, or a Mind Map.
  Highlight key points in colour.

- **Re-read** the spread after a break of 5–10 minutes.

- **Take care** : read the 'Take care' box.
  Can you see how you can use this advice?

- ✓ **Tick and date** the pull-out Revision Calendar.

2. Practise

- **Try** the questions on the double-page of questions.
  These are in the same style as the ones in the exam.

- **Check** your answers. The answers begin on page 108.
  Read the Examiners' Hints carefully.
  Go back over anything you find difficult.

- ✓ **Tick and date** the pull-out Revision Calendar to
  keep a record of your progress.

Then later:

Re-visit
Re-visit each topic 1 day later, and then 1 week later.
Read the double-page spread, your notes or Mind Map,
and the questions you answered.

Up your Grade
At the end of each section of topics, read the Sample
Answers at Grade A and Grade C.
Look at the Hints and Tips for improving your grade.

Top-up
Use the Revision Cards to remind you of the key points,
and test yourself.
Even better, make your own Revision Cards.

Examination Technique

Before the exam

1. Make sure you know the dates and times of all your exams, so that you are not late!
   See the table at the bottom of this page.

2. Make sure you know which topics are going to be examined on which paper.

3. On the night before the exam, it may help to do some quick revision – but don't do too much.
   Make sure you get a good night's sleep.

On the day of the exam

1. Aim to arrive early at the exam room.

2. Make sure that you are properly equipped with pens and pencils (including spares), an eraser, a ruler, a calculator (check the battery!) and a watch.

During the exam

1. Don't waste time when you get the paper. Write your name and candidate number (unless they are already printed).
   Read the instructions on the front page of the booklet, carefully, and make sure you follow them.

2. Read each question very carefully.
   In each question there is always a 'command' word that tells you what to do.
   If the question says '**State ...**' or '**List ...**' or '**Name ...**' then you should give a short answer.
   If the question says '**Explain ...**' or '**Describe ...**' or '**Why does ...**' or '**Suggest ...**' then you should make sure you give a longer answer.

   Put a ring round each 'command' word.

   Then underline the key words in the question.
   For example:

   Calculate the potential difference across a 5 Ω resistor when a current of 2 A is passing.

   Then you can see exactly what is given to you in the question, and what you have to do.

   Make sure that you answer only the question shown on the exam paper (not the one that you wish had been asked).

Here is one way of collecting information about all your exams (in all your subjects):

Date, time and room	Subject, paper number and tier	Length (hours)	Types of question: – structured? – single word answers? – longer answers? – essays?	Sections?	Details of choice (if any)	Approximate time per mark (minutes)
5th June 9.30 Hall	Science (Double Award) Paper 3 (Physics) Higher Tier	1½	Structured questions (with single-word answers and longer answers)	1	no choice	1 min.

Answering the questions

Structured questions

- Make sure you know exactly what the question is asking.

- Look for the number of marks awarded for each part of the question. For example *(2 marks)* means that the Examiner will expect 2 main (and different) points in your answer.

- The number of lines of space is also a guide to how much you are expected to write.

- Make sure that you use any data provided in the question.

- Pace yourself with a watch so that you don't run out of time. You should aim to use 1 minute for each mark. So if a question has 3 marks it should take you about 3 minutes.

- In calculations, show all the steps in your working. This way you may get marks for the way you tackle the problem, even if your final answer is wrong. Make sure that you put the correct units on the answer.

- Try to write something for each part of every question.

- Follow the instructions given in the question. If it asks for one answer, give only one answer.

- If you have spare time at the end, use it wisely.

Extended questions

- Some questions require longer answers, where you will need to write two or more full sentences.

- The questions may include the words '***Describe***...' or '***Explain***...' or '***Evaluate***...' or '***Suggest***...' or '***Why does***...'.

- Make sure that the sentences are in good English and are linked to each other.

- Make sure you use scientific words in your answer.

- As before, the marks and the number of lines will give you a guide to how much to write. Make sure you include enough detail with at least as many points as there are marks.

- For the highest grades you need to include full details, in scientific language, written in good English, and with the sentences linking together in the correct sequence.

For multiple-choice questions:
- Read the instructions carefully.
- Mark the answer sheet exactly as you are instructed.
- If you have to rub out an answer, make sure that you rub it out well, so no pencil mark is left.
- Even if the answer looks obvious, look at all the alternatives before making a decision.
- If you are not sure of the answer, then first delete any answers that look wrong.
- If you still don't know the answer, then make an educated guess!
- Ensure that you give an answer to every question.

1 CONDUCTION
CONVECTION
RADIATION

> ▶ **ThinkAbout:**
>
> 1. When a hot object is touching a cold object, energy is transferred from the . . . . object to the . . . . object.
> 2. Heat can be transferred by conduction, ..., and . . . .
> 3. Metals are . . . . conductors. Non-metals are usually poor . . . .
> 4. Air and other gases are . . . . conductors. They are good . . . .
> 5. Heat can also be called . . . . energy.

> ▶ **Conduction**
>
> Conduction is the transfer of energy through a substance without the substance itself moving.
>
> At the hot end the atoms are vibrating with more kinetic energy, and this energy is gradually passed along the bar.
>
> Non-metals, liquids and gases are usually poor conductors. Metals are very good conductors.

H

> Metals are very good conductors because they have a lot of free electrons that can move through the metal.
>
> The electrons diffuse through the metal structure and collide with other electrons and the metal ions, so they transfer energy to the colder parts.

Ways of reducing the heat loss from a house

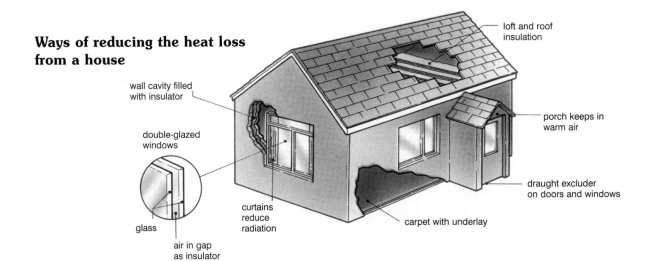

- loft and roof insulation
- wall cavity filled with insulator
- porch keeps in warm air
- double-glazed windows
- draught excluder on doors and windows
- glass
- curtains reduce radiation
- carpet with underlay
- air in gap as insulator

▶ Convection

Liquids and gases can flow, and so they can transfer energy from hot places to colder places.

Warm air is less dense and rises

Cold air is more dense, and falls

> **H**
>
> The particles in the liquid or gas (fluid) move faster when they are hot. The fluid expands.
>
> The warm regions are then **less dense** than the cold regions. So the warm regions rise, and the colder regions replace the warmer regions.

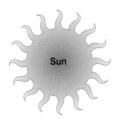
Sun

▶ Radiation

The hotter an object is, the more energy it radiates, like the Sun.

Hot objects emit mainly infra red radiation.
The energy is transferred by waves (see Topic 16).
Particles of matter are **not** involved.

Emitting

For surfaces at the same temperature, a dark, matt surface **emits more** energy than a light shiny surface.
e.g. this is why kettles are shiny, to stay hot.
e.g. the warm pipes at the back of a fridge are black, to lose energy.

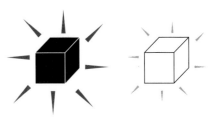

Absorbing

A dark matt surface is also a good absorber of radiation energy (because it is a poor reflector).
e.g. this is why solar panels are matt black, to absorb as much energy as possible.

A light, shiny surface is a better reflector, so it is a poor absorber.
e.g. this is why fire-fighting suits are shiny.

Take care:

• Don't confuse the words **conduction** and **convection**.

• Remember they both involve particles, but **radiation** does not.

• Don't confuse the words **emission** and **absorption**.

More details in **Physics for You**, pages 42–53, 219, 221, 227.

Examination Questions – Conduction, Convection, Radiation
Module Test Questions

1 The fire-fighter is dressed in a shiny, white, fire-retarding suit.

Which **two** statements explain the reasons for choosing shiny, white suits rather than matt, black suits?

A   matt, black suits are good absorbers of radiation

B   matt, black suits are good reflectors of radiation

C   shiny, white suits are good absorbers of radiation

D   shiny, white suits are good conductors of thermal energy

E   shiny, white suits are good reflectors of radiation

H 2 Different types of thermal energy transfer are explained in different ways.
Match words from the list with the spaces **1–4** in the sentences.

density

free electrons

kinetic energy

waves

When a substance becomes hotter, its particles have greater ...... **1**...... .

Conduction in metals occurs because of the movement of ...... **2**...... .

Convection occurs in a fluid because of differences in ....**3**....... .

Radiation occurs by means of ...... **4**....... .

H 3 Energy is transferred by several different methods.

Match words from the list with the spaces **1–4** in the sentences.

collisions

electrons

ions

waves

In metals, energy is moved to cooler regions by free ....**1**...... .

Energy is transferred by ....**2**...... between these and ....**3**......

Energy is transferred from a hot metal through space by ...... **4**......

10
marks

Terminal Paper Questions

1 The diagram shows how heat escapes from a house.

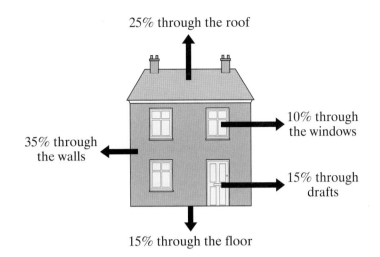

25% through the roof

10% through the windows

35% through the walls

15% through drafts

15% through the floor

(a) (i) Through which part of this house is most heat lost?

....

(1 mark)

(ii) Complete the sentence below.

The amount of heat lost through the floor can be **reduced** by fitting ....

....

(1 mark)

(iii) Complete the sentence below.

The amount of heat lost through the windows can be **reduced** by fitting

....

(1 mark)

(b) The table shows the cost of fitting various things to reduce heat loss from the house.
It also shows the money saved each year when they have been fitted.

Fitting	Cost	Money saved per year
Cavity wall insulation	£450	£250
Draught-proofing	£25	£50
Double-glazing	£1200	£60
Loft insulation	£150	£100

Using the information given in the table, explain which is the most cost-effective thing
to fit.

....

....

....

....

(3 marks)

6 marks

Answers on page 108

Using electricity

▶ **ThinkAbout:**

1. Movement energy is also called . . . . energy.
   Heat is also called . . . . energy.
2. A kettle transfers electrical . . . . to . . . .
   energy.
3. An electric lamp transfers . . . . energy to
   . . . . and . . . . energy.
4. A loudspeaker transfers . . . . energy to
   . . . . energy.
5. An electric motor transfers . . . . energy to
   . . . . energy.
6. A hairdryer transfers . . . . energy to . . . .,
   . . . . and . . . . energy.

▶ **Electrical energy**

Electrical energy is very convenient, and easily
transferred to heat, light, sound and kinetic energy
in your home.
(For other forms of energy see also Topic 3.)

How much electrical energy is transferred by an appliance
depends on:
* how much time the appliance is switched on,
* how fast the appliance transfers energy (its **power**).
  The power is measured in watts (W) or kilowatts (kW).
  1 kW = 1000 W

If the energy is measured in kilowatt-hours, called Units,
then the formula is:

energy transferred	=	**power**	×	**time**
(kilowatt-hour, kWh, Unit)		(kilowatt, kW)		(hour, h)

The cost of this energy is found by:

total cost	=	**number of Units (kWh)**	×	**cost per Unit**

Example 1

A 2 kW electric fire is switched on for 5 hours.
What is the cost, at 8p per Unit?

energy transferred = power × time
                   = 2 kW × 5 h
                   = 10 kWh = 10 Units

cost = number of Units × cost per Unit
     = 10 Units × 8p per Unit
     = 80 pence

Example 2

The number of Units
can be found by reading
an electricity meter:

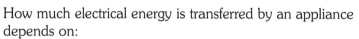
before

Can you see that the
energy transferred is 10 Units?

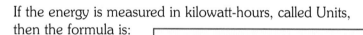
after

If the energy is measured in joules (J),
then use watts and seconds:

energy transferred	=	**power**	×	**time**
(joules, J)		(watt, W)		(second, s)

▶ Power

Power is a measure of how fast the energy is transferred.
The greater the power, the more energy is transferred in a given time.

power (in watts, W) = $\dfrac{\textbf{energy transferred} \ \text{(in joules, J)}}{\textbf{time taken} \ \text{(in seconds, s)}}$

1 watt is the rate of transferring 1 joule in 1 second.

More details in
Physics for You,
pages 272–273,
266–267.

Example

A 100 W lamp is switched on for 2 hours.
How much energy is transferred to the room?

$$\text{power} \quad = \quad \frac{\text{energy transferred}}{\text{time taken}}$$

$$100\,\text{W} \quad = \quad \frac{\text{energy transferred}}{2 \times 60 \times 60 \ \text{seconds}}$$

$$\therefore \quad \text{energy transferred} \quad = \quad 100\,\text{W} \times 2 \times 60 \times 60 \ \text{seconds}$$

$$= \quad \underline{720\,000 \ \text{joules}} \quad (= 720 \ \text{kJ})$$

▶ Heating a resistor

An electric current is a flow of charge.
When the charge flows through a resistor, electrical energy is transferred as heat (e.g. in a lamp).

The rate of energy transfer (the power) is given by:

power   =   **potential difference**   ×   **current**
(watt, W)   (volt, V)   (ampere, A)

Example

In the circuit shown, what is
the power of the lamp?

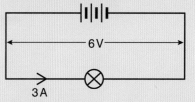

power = p.d. × current
        = 6 V × 3 A
        = <u>18 W</u> (18 joules/sec)

If the voltage (p.d.) is higher and the charge is bigger,
then more energy is transferred, because:

energy transferred   =   **p. d.**   ×   **charge**
(joule, J)   (volt, V)   (coulomb, C)

The amount of charge is given by:

charge   =   **current**   ×   **time**
(coulomb, C)   (ampere, A)   (seconds, s)

Example

In the circuit shown above, how much charge flows
in 10 seconds?

charge   =   current × time
        =   3 A × 10 s   =   <u>30 coulomb</u> (30 C)

Take care:

Notice that
joules, watts
and seconds
go together,
while Units
(kWh), kilowatts and hours
go together.

Examination Questions – Using electricity

Module Test Questions

1 These devices are designed to transfer electrical energy.

Match words from the list with the spaces **1–4** in the sentences.

heat (thermal energy)

light

movement (kinetic energy)

sound

The fan is designed to transfer electrical energy as ...... **1**........ .

The iron is designed to transfer electrical energy as ...... **2**...... .

The lamp is designed to transfer electrical energy as ...... **3**...... .

The loudspeaker is designed to transfer electrical energy as ...... **4**...... .

2 A drill usefully transfers some of the energy that is supplied to it. The rest of the energy is wasted.

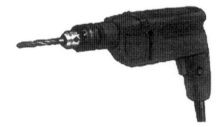

D **2.1** The drill has a power of 500 W.
Every second the drill transfers …

    A 500 J

    B 500 kW

    C 500 kWh

    D 500 W

2.2 The drill usefully transfers energy as …

    A heat (thermal energy).

    B light.

    C movement (kinetic energy).

    D sound.

6
marks

Terminal Paper Questions

D 1 A student irons for 30 minutes. The power of the iron is 1.5 kW.

(a) How many Units of electrical energy are transferred by the iron during this time?

....

Number of Units = ...

(1 mark)

(b) How many watts are there in 1.5 kW?

....

Number of watts = ...

(1 mark)

(c) How many seconds are in 30 minutes?

....

Number of seconds = ...

(1 mark)

(d) How many joules of electrical energy are transferred by the iron during this time?

....

Number of joules = ...

(1 mark)

2 Here are the readings on an electricity meter:

Date	Meter reading
1st January	38017
1st April	39984

(a) How many Units of electricity were used between 1st January and 1st April?

....

Number of Units = ...

(1 mark)

(b) One Unit of electricity costs 8p. What is the total cost, in £ of this electricity?

....

Cost = ...

(1 mark)

D 3 A lamp is connected to a 230 V supply. The current in the lamp is 0.25 A.
H
(a) How much charge flows through the lamp in 1 hour?

....

....

Charge = ... C

(3 marks)

(b) How much energy is transferred by the lamp in 1 hour?

....

....

Energy transferred = ... J

(2 marks)

11
marks

15

3 Energy transfers

▶ **Forms of energy**

Energy can exist as heat (thermal energy), sound, light (radiant), electrical, movement (kinetic), nuclear, gravitational potential energy, elastic potential energy, and chemical (food/fuel) energy.

It is measured in joules (J).

In the diagram, gravitational potential energy (PE) is being transferred to kinetic energy (KE).
(To calculate gravitational PE, see Topic 12.)

The total energy is constant

▶ **Energy Transfer Diagrams**

Here is an Energy Transfer Diagram for a torch:

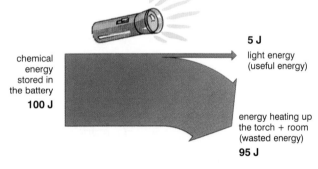

chemical energy stored in the battery
100 J

5 J light energy (useful energy)

energy heating up the torch + room (wasted energy)
95 J

As you can see, the **total** amount of energy is constant. (100 J = 5 J + 95 J)

Although there is the same amount of energy afterwards, **not all of it is useful**.

Eventually both the 'useful' energy and the 'wasted' energy are transferred to the surroundings, which become warmer.

Law 1 (the law of conservation of energy)
The total amount of energy is constant ('conserved').
Energy cannot be created or destroyed.

Law 2 (the law of spreading of energy)
In energy transfers, the energy spreads out, to more and more places.
As it spreads, it becomes less useful to us.

▶ Efficiency

In the torch diagram on the opposite page,
for every 100 joules of energy input to the bulb,
only 5 joules are output as *useful* light energy.
The rest is wasted.
We say the **efficiency** is $\frac{5}{100}$ or 0.05 or 5%.

The definition of efficiency is:

$$\text{efficiency} = \frac{\text{useful energy output}}{\text{total energy input}}$$

Example 1

What is the efficiency of this modern
'energy-saver' light bulb?

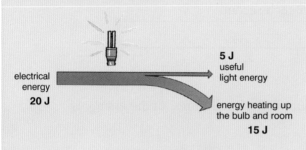

electrical energy 20 J

5 J useful light energy

energy heating up the bulb and room 15 J

$$\text{efficiency} = \frac{\text{useful energy output}}{\text{total energy input}}$$

$$= \frac{5}{20}$$

$$= \underline{0.25} \text{ or } \underline{25\%}$$

Example 2

A kettle is supplied
with 180 000 joules
of electrical energy,
but 18 000 joules
are lost to the
surroundings.
What is the efficiency of the kettle in heating
the water?

$$\text{useful energy} = 180\,000 \text{ J} - 18\,000 \text{ J}$$

$$= 162\,000 \text{ J}$$

$$\text{efficiency} = \frac{\text{useful energy output}}{\text{total energy input}}$$

$$= \frac{162\,000 \text{ J}}{180\,000 \text{ J}}$$

$$= \underline{0.9} \text{ or } \underline{90\%}$$

Example 3

A solar panel has an efficiency of 15% (= 0.15).
What is its electrical output if the input is 200 W?

In 1 second, the input is 200 joules.

$$\text{efficiency} = \frac{\text{useful energy output}}{\text{total energy input}}$$

$$0.15 = \frac{\text{useful energy output}}{200 \text{ J}}$$

$$\text{so useful energy output} = 0.15 \times 200 \text{ J}$$

$$= 30 \text{ J in 1 second}$$

$$\text{so power output} = \underline{30 \text{ W}}$$

Take care:

- There are no units
  for efficiency.
  It is just a number
  (e.g. 0.8 or 80%)

- Exam questions may ask you
  to suggest ways of reducing
  wasteful energy transfers.

More details in *Physics for You*, pages 109–112, 122.

Examination Questions – Energy transfers

Module Test Questions

1   The diagram shows a 100 watt (W) lamp.

It sends out light at a rate of 5 watts.

Match numbers from the list with the spaces **1–4** in the table.

   0.05 (5%)

   5 J

   95 J

   100 J

1	amount of energy supplied to the lamp each second
2	amount of energy transferred as light each second
3	amount of energy wasted each second
4	efficiency of the lamp

2   A drill usefully transfers some of the energy that is supplied to it. The rest of the energy is wasted.

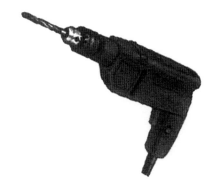

2.1   Some of the energy transferred to the drill is wasted as …

   A   heat (thermal energy) only.

   B   heat (thermal energy) and sound energy.

   C   movement (kinetic energy) and light energy.

   D   movement (kinetic energy) and sound energy.

2.2   The energy that is wasted by the drill …

   A   can easily be used for other useful energy transfers.

   B   eventually disappears.

   C   is easy to recycle.

   D   is eventually transferred to the surroundings.

6
marks

Terminal Paper Questions

1 The diagram shows a solar powered fountain.

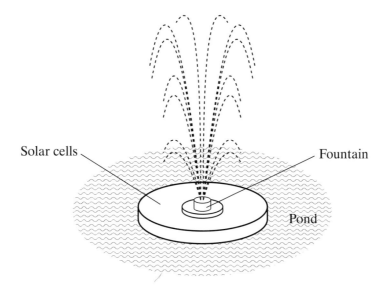

A motor pumps water from the pond to the fountain.

The solar cells power the motor.

(a) Complete each sentence by choosing the correct words from the box.

chemical	**electrical**	**gravitational potential**	**heat (thermal)**
	light	**movement (kinetic)**	**sound**

(i) The solar cells transfer .... energy to electrical energy.

(1 mark)

(ii) The motor is designed to transfer .... energy to

.... energy.

(2 marks)

(iii) As the water rises, kinetic energy is transferred to ....

energy.

(1 mark)

(b) Name **one** form of wasted energy which is transferred when the motor is running.

.... energy

(1 mark)

5 marks

Answers on page 109

4 Energy resources

> **ThinkAbout:**
>
> 1. Coal, gas, oil and wood are all . . . . They release . . . . when they are burned.
> 2. Coal, oil and gas are called . . . . fuels. Fossil fuels and nuclear fuels are called non- . . . . energy resources.
> 3. Once fosssil fuels are used up, they can . . . . be replaced for million years.
> 4. Wood is a . . . . energy resource. Other renewable resources are . . . . and . . . . and . . . .

> ## Generating electricity in power stations

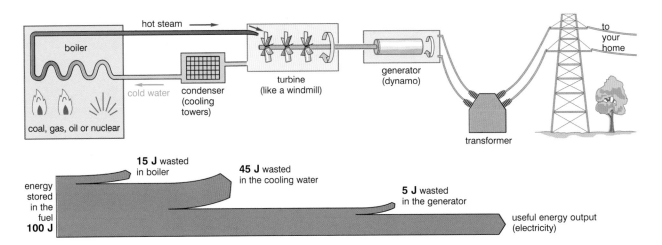

Energy from a fuel is used to heat water.
Fuels include:
- fossil fuels (e.g. gas, oil, coal),
- nuclear fuels (e.g. uranium, plutonium).

The steam which is produced is used to turn turbines.
The turbines then drive generators, which produce electricity (see Topic 9).

> ## Generating electricity from renewable energy resources
>
> Energy from renewable resources can be used to drive turbines directly, using:
> - the wind (e.g. a wind generator or a windmill),
> - the rise and fall of water due to waves,
> - the flow of falling water from a hydroelectric dam, or a tidal barrage.
>
> In some volcanic areas, hot water or steam may rise near to the surface.
> The steam can be tapped and used to drive a turbine.
> This geothermal energy originally came from the decay of radioactive elements (e.g. uranium) within the Earth.
>
> Electricity can be produced directly from the Sun's radiation, using a solar cell.

Answers:

1. fuels, energy   2. fossil, renewable   3. not   4. renewable, sunlight/wind/waves/falling water/tides

▶ Effect on the environment

Using different energy sources has different effects on the environment.

These effects include:
- possible global warming, due to the greenhouse effect, due to CO_2 emissions,
- acid rain, due to SO_2 emissions,
- radioactive leaks and waste,
- damage to the local ecology.

See the table below.

▶ Availability

Energy sources also differ in when they can become available, to supply a demand for electricity.

Ideally they should have a short start-up time, so that they can respond quickly to a surge in demand.

See the table below.

▶ Comparing power stations

Power station	Disadvantages:	Advantages:
Coal-fired Oil-fired	• emits CO_2, so it increases greenhouse effect • emits SO_2, and so causes acid rain • limited fuel available	• coal will be the last fossil fuel to run out
Gas-fired	• emits CO_2 (but less than coal) • limited fuel available	• quick start-up if there's a sudden demand
Nuclear	• needs disposal of nuclear waste, safely • risk of big accident, like Chernobyl • limited fuel available	• does not produce CO_2 or SO_2, so does not increase greenhouse effect or make acid rain
Wind (turbine)	• needs many large turbines • unsightly, noisy • unreliable, wind does not blow every day	• free energy resource • no air pollution
Hydroelecric (dam)	• impossible in flat or dry regions • floods a large area, affects ecology • expensive to build	• quick to start up if a sudden demand • reliable energy source (in wet regions) • can be used in reverse to store energy • free energy resource • no air pollution
Tidal (barrage)	• needs a place with high tides • affects the ecology of the area • very expensive to build	• reliable (but the tides may not be at the right time for the demand) • free energy resource • no air pollution
Solar cell	• very high cost per Unit of electricity • unreliable (because dependent on weather and daylight)	• good for remote locations (e.g. deserts, satellites) or for small amounts of electricity (e.g. watches, calculators) • free energy resource • no air pollution

More details in **_Physics for You_**, pages 11–13, 113–115.

Take care:

To get full marks in exam questions, you may need to refer to more than one advantage / disadvantage.

Examination Questions – Energy resources

Module Test Questions

1 The diagram shows four different ways of generating electricity.

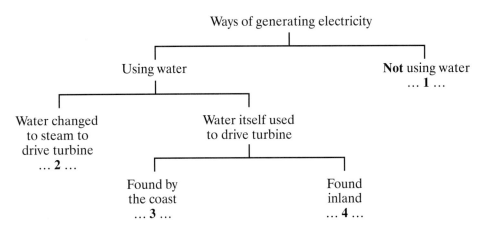

Match words from the list with the numbers **1–4** on the diagram.

hydroelectric dam

nuclear power station

solar cells

tidal barrage

2 Electricity can be generated from different energy resources.

Match each resource from the list with the numbers **1–4** in the table.

coal

geothermal

hydroelectric

uranium

Energy resource	How the resource is used in power stations
1	used as the fuel in a nuclear power station
2	burned in a conventional power station
3	uses energy released in volcanic areas
4	uses liquid water to drive turbines

3 The radioactive substances that are found in the Earth's crust can release energy.

Which **two** of the following make use of this energy?

fossil fuels

geothermal energy sources

nuclear power stations

tidal barrages

solar cells

10 marks

Terminal Paper Questions

1 Electricity is a useful form of energy.

Different energy sources can be used to generate electricity.

Wind is an energy source	Coal, a fossil fuel, is an energy source
Wind → Electrical energy	Coal (containing some sulphur) → Power station → Electrical energy
This wind turbine generates 1 MW. (1 MW = 1000 kW)	This coal-fired power station generates 1000 MW.
Electricity demand in the UK can be 48 000 MW.	

Give **one** advantage and **one** disadvantage (other than cost) of using each energy source to generate electricity in the UK.

Advantage	Disadvantage
Using wind	Using wind ....
Using coal	Using coal ....

(*4 marks*)

4 marks

Answers on page 109

Getting the Grades – Energy

Try this question, then compare your answer with the two examples opposite ▶

1 The graph shows the expected change in the world demand for energy.
It also shows how the supplies of various energy resources are expected to change.

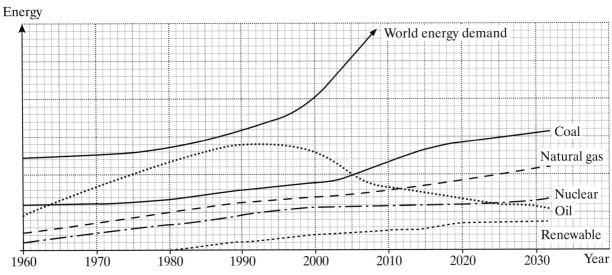

Energy

1960   1970   1980   1990   2000   2010   2020   2030   Year

(a) The supply of energy from oil is decreasing. The supply from coal is increasing.

   (i) Why is this a problem for the environment?

   .... *(1 mark)*

   (ii) Use the graph to estimate when supplies from oil and coal will be equal. .... *(1 mark)*

(b) We have relied on fossil fuels to supply most of our energy needs.
Use the graph to explain why:

   (i) there could be a supply problem in the future:

   .... *(1 mark)*

   (ii) we must find alternative energy resources.

   .... *(1 mark)*

(c) On average, the energy use of each family in the UK releases over 25 tonnes of carbon dioxide
and 4 kilograms of sulphur dioxide into the air every year.

   (i) State one environmental effect which is increased by releasing carbon dioxide into the atmosphere.

   .... *(1 mark)*

   (ii) State a different environmental effect caused by releasing sulphur dioxide into the atmosphere.

   .... *(1 mark)*

(d) Electricity can be generated using nuclear fuels. Apart from the cost of electricity, what are the
advantages and disadvantages of doing this?

   ....

   .... *(5 marks)*

GRADE 'A' ANSWER

Jessica has scored both marks. She gives a complete answer to the first part and correctly reads the graph for the second part.

Jessica has understood the relationship between energy demand and energy supply and has mentioned both of these in her answer.

Jessica correctly answers both parts of the question.

Jessica

(a) (i) coal produces more CO_2 than oil ✓
    (ii) 2005 ✓
(b) (i) The World demand for energy is rising rapidly. ✓
    (ii) Fossil fuels will run out over the next two hundred years, so there will not be enough resources to meet the future demand ✓
(c) (i) Greenhouse effect causing the Earth to get warmer. ✓
    (ii) acid rain ✓
(d)   There is plenty of nuclear fuel in the world. ✓ Nuclear power stations do not burn fuels so no waste gases are produced. ✓ Nuclear fuels are radioactive and need to be handled very carefully. ✓ Waste nuclear fuel remains very reactive for a long time and has to be stored away from people. ✓ Nuclear fuels won't run out for a long time. Nuclear fuel can be very unsafe.

Jessica has made four valid points but her last points are really saying the same thing as her previous points so she does not get any extra credit for them.
She could have gained more marks by saying that very little radiation escapes when a nuclear power station is running normally, or that a nuclear power station takes a long time to start up.

10 marks = Grade A answer

▶ **Improve your Grades   A up to A***

To get an A* you must be able to argue a clear case without repeating yourself. If there are 5 marks available you must make 5 clear points. You must remember to include both advantages and disadvantages to gain all the marks.

GRADE 'C' ANSWER

Michael does not get any marks because he has not answered the question. Burning oil and coal both cause atmospheric pollution. Michael needs to say that coal produces more CO_2 than oil for the same energy.

Michael scores the first mark, but his answer to the second part is incomplete. He should say that there will not be enough fossil fuels to meet the demand in the future.

Michael has seen the word 'disadvantages' and has answered accordingly. However, he has forgotten to give any advantages so he cannot gain more than 3 marks. Michael scores 3 of the 5 marks.

Michael

(a) (i) Burning coal causes pollution ✗
    (ii) 2005 ✓

(b) (i) The demand for energy is increasing ✓
    (ii) Soon there will not be enough ✗

(c) (i) Damages the ozone layer ✗
    (ii) Acid rain ✓

(d)   Nuclear radiation is dangerous If radioactive substances escape into the environment they will kill things. ✓ The waste is radioactive ✓ Radioactive waste has to be stored underground. ✓ It takes a long time to start it up.

Michael has read correctly from the graph and scores the mark.

Michael is confused between different problems caused by atmospheric pollution and the first answer is incorrect.

6 marks = Grade C answer

▶ **Improve your Grades   C up to B**

Grade C candidates often fail to get marks because they do not read the questions carefully enough. Make sure that you give a complete answer to each part of the question.

---

5 CIRCUITS

▷ **ThinkAbout:**

1. A current is a flow of . . . .
2. Current is measured in units called . . . .
3. If the same current goes through 2 components, they are in . . . .
4. An ammeter is always placed in . . . .
5. Another name for voltage is . . . .
6. A voltmeter is always placed in . . . .
7. Resistance is measured in . . . .
8. All metals are good . . . . because they have a lot of free . . . .

▷ **Circuit Symbols to remember:**

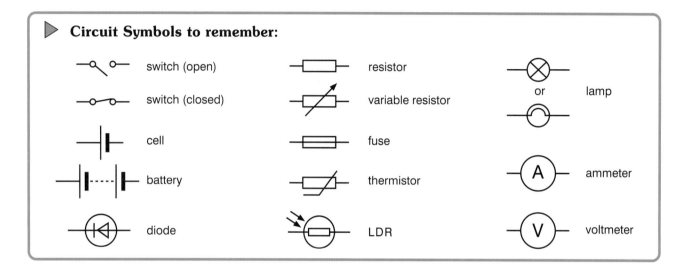

switch (open)	resistor	lamp (or)
switch (closed)	variable resistor	
cell	fuse	ammeter (A)
battery	thermistor	
diode	LDR	voltmeter (V)

▷ **Resistors in series**

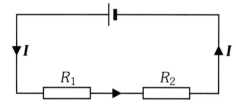

- The same current I goes through all the components.

- The potential difference across the cell is shared between the 2 resistors.

- The larger resistance has the larger p.d. across it.

- In the diagram above, total resistance, $R = R_1 + R_2$

▷ **Resistors in parallel**

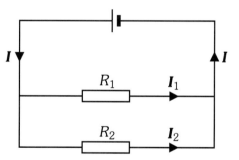

- The p.d. across R_1 is equal to the p.d. across R_2 (and equal to the p.d. of the cell).

- The current I from the cell is shared between the 2 branches.

- The larger resistance has the smaller current through it.

- In the diagram above, total current, $I = I_1 + I_2$

▷ Current : voltage graphs

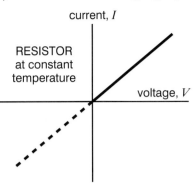

current, *I*

RESISTOR
at constant
temperature

voltage, *V*

current, *I*

a
filament
LAMP

voltage, *V*

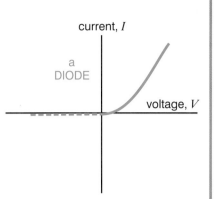

current, *I*

a
DIODE

voltage, *V*

If a resistor is kept at constant temperature, the **current I** through it is proportional to the **voltage V** across the resistor.

When a current flows through the lamp, it gets hotter, and so its resistance increases ... and so the curve bends as shown.

In a diode, the current can flow one way only.
It has a very high resistance in the reverse direction.

The dotted part of the graph shows what happens when you reverse the voltage.

LDR, Light-Dependent Resistor

As more light shines on this resistor, its resistance decreases, so that more current flows.

Thermistor

When this resistor gets hotter, its resistance decreases, so that more current flows.

▷ Potential difference V, current I, and resistance R

potential difference, *V*	=	current, *I*	×	resistance, *R*
(in volts, V)		(in amps, A)		(in ohms, Ω)

$$V = I \times R$$

Example

What is the current in this circuit?

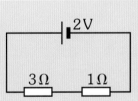

2 V

3 Ω   1 Ω

Total resistance $= 3\,\Omega + 1\,\Omega = 4\,\Omega$

$$V = I \times R$$

$$2\,V = I \times 4\,\Omega$$

so $I = \frac{1}{2}$ amp $= \underline{0.5\,A}$

Take care:

- Make sure you are clear about the differences between series and parallel circuits.

- Ammeters are always in series, voltmeters always in parallel.

- Make sure you include units (volts, amps or ohms) in your calculations.

- Learn all the circuit symbols.

More details in **Physics for You**, pages 254–265, 325.

Examination Questions – Circuits

Module Test Questions

1 The diagram shows a simple electric circuit. Match words from the list with each of the symbols **1–4** on the diagram.

> **diode**
>
> **fuse**
>
> **resistor**
>
> **switch**

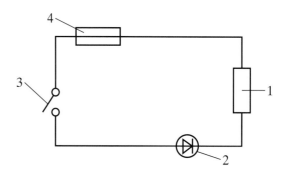

2 Components in circuits do different things.

Match each component from the list with its description **1–4** in the table.

> **cell**
>
> **diode**
>
> **LDR**
>
> **switch**

Component	Description
1	allows a current to flow in one direction only
2	its resistance depends on light intensity
3	provides the voltage in a circuit
4	opens or closes an electrical circuit

3 The graph shows what happens to the current through component **X** when the potential difference (p.d.) across it is varied.

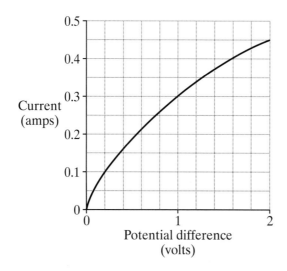

The p.d. across component **X** is increased from 1 volt to 2 volts.

Which **two** of the following statements are **false**?

> **A** component X could be a filament lamp
>
> **B** the current also doubles
>
> **C** the current increases to less than double
>
> **D** the resistance of component X decreases
>
> **E** the resistance of component X increases

10
marks

Terminal Paper Questions

1 The drawing shows an electric toaster which takes a current of 3 A from the 230 V mains supply.

(a) Calculate the resistance of the heating element.

....

....

....

....

Resistance = ... ohms

(2 marks)

(b) The drawing shows a hair dryer designed to run from the 230 V mains supply.

The resistance of the device is 45 ohms.

Calculate the current taken from the mains.

....

....

....

....

Current = ... A

(2 marks)

4 marks

Answers on page 110

MAGNETIC effect of a current

> ### ThinkAbout:

1. The end of a magnetic compass which points North is called the . . . .-seeking pole or . . . .-pole.
2. Like poles . . . . , unlike poles . . . .
3. The direction of a magnetic field is shown by . . . . of flux. The lines point from the . . . .-pole to the . . . .-pole.
4. A magnet exerts a . . . . on any magnetic material (e.g. . . . .) which is nearby.
5. A coil of wire acts like a bar . . . . when an electric . . . . flows through it. This is called an . . . .
6. If the current in an electromagnet is reversed, the . . . . are reversed.

> ### Magnetic fields

The field round a bar magnet and round an electromagnet have the same shape:

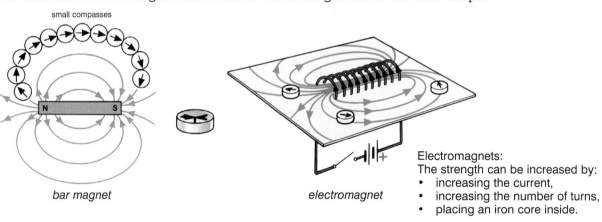

small compasses

bar magnet

electromagnet

Electromagnets:
The strength can be increased by:
• increasing the current,
• increasing the number of turns,
• placing an iron core inside.

> ### The motor effect

D

If a wire carrying a current cuts across a magnetic field, it experiences a force on it.

The size of the force can be increased by:
• increasing the current,
• increasing the strength of the magnetic field.
The direction of the force will be reversed if the direction of *either* the current *or* the field is reversed.

This effect is used in electric motors, circuit-breakers, etc (see the opposite page).

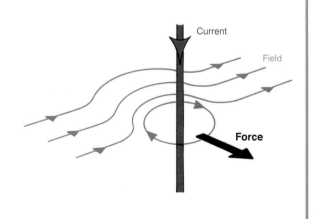

Current

Field

Force

▷ The electric motor

In the diagram, the electric motor has:
- a permanent magnet,
- a coil through which a current is flowing.

Because of the motor effect (see the opposite page), each side of the coil has a force on it. The force is **up** on one side and **down** on the other.

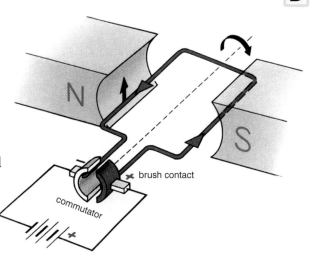

The motor can be made more powerful by:
- increasing the current,
- increasing the number of turns on the coil,
- using a stronger magnet.

▷ A circuit-breaker

A circuit-breaker is a safety device, like a fuse. It should cut off the current if too much current flows.
The diagram shows one kind of circuit-breaker:

If a large current flows, the iron bar is pulled to the electromagnet, and this breaks the circuit.

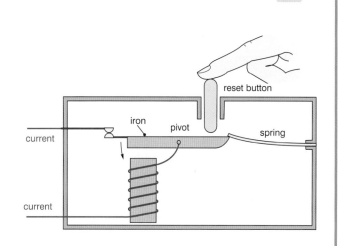

Like a fuse, a circuit-breaker should only be put in the live wire.
It is easier to use than a fuse, because it is easily re-set.

Electromagnets are also used in metal scrapyards, eye hospitals, electric bells, relays and loudspeakers.

Take care:

If you are shown a diagram of a circuit-breaker different from the one shown above, then analyse it to see:

– where is the electromagnet?
– which parts can move?
– how can this break the circuit?

Then you can explain how it works, step by step.

More details in **Physics for You**, pages 292–301, 312.

Examination Questions – Magnetic effect of a current
Module Test Questions

D **1** The diagram shows some of the parts of a d.c. motor.

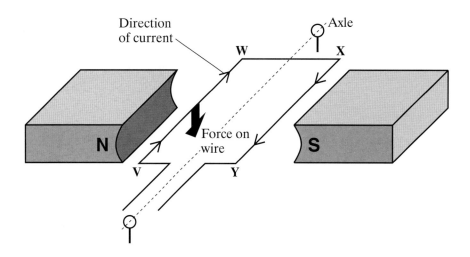

1.1 The direction of the force acting on side **XY** of the coil is …

A   downwards.

B   from **X** to **Y**.

C   from **Y** to **X**.

D   upwards.

1.2 The overall effect of the forces acting on the coil is …

A   to have no effect because they are balanced.

B   to move the coil upwards.

C   to rotate the coil anticlockwise ⌒.

D   to rotate the coil clockwise ⌒.

1.3 Instead of passing a current through the coil, the coil is rotated.
The device is then acting as …

A   an a.c. motor.

B   a circuit breaker.

C   a generator.

D   a transformer.

3
marks

Terminal Paper Questions

D **1** The diagram shows a simple electric motor.

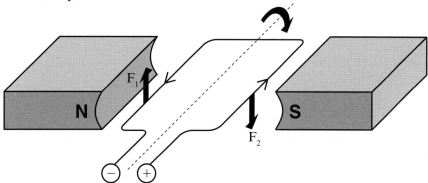

The coil turns as shown in the diagram.

(a) State **two** ways of reversing the direction of forces **F₁** and **F₂**.

1. ....

....

2. ....

....

(2 marks)

(b) Give **two** ways in which the size of the forces can be increased.

1. ....

....

2. ....

....

(2 marks)

D **2** The diagram shows a circuit breaker.

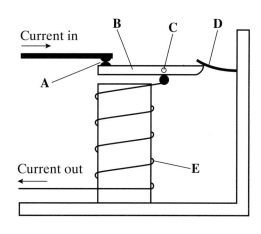

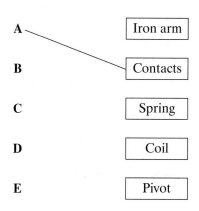

The letters on the left correspond to the labels on the diagram.

The boxes on the right give the correct names to the parts shown on the diagram.

Draw a straight line from each letter to the correct name. One has been done for you.

(4 marks)

8
marks

Answers on page 110

7

STATIC ELECTRICITY

▷ **ThinkAbout:**

1. There are two kinds of charge, called positive and . . . .
2. Insulators can be . . . . by rubbing them.
3. Electrons have a . . . . charge.

4. Negative charges repel other . . . . charges.
5. An object that gains electrons becomes . . . . charged. An object that loses electrons becomes . . . . charged.

D

▷ **Charging an insulator by rubbing**

In the diagram, when the polythene strip is rubbed with wool, electrons are rubbed off the wool and move on to the polythene (which becomes negative).

The wool is short of electrons, so it is positive.

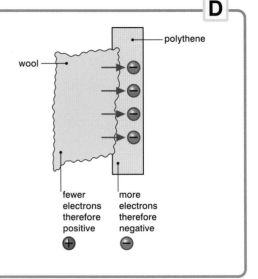

polythene

wool

fewer electrons therefore positive

more electrons therefore negative

Like charges repel.
Unlike charges attract.

H

▷ **Sparks**

The more charge put on an object, the higher the voltage (potential difference) between the object and earth.
If the potential difference is very high, then a spark can jump between the object and any earthed conductor. This can be dangerous.
For example, pipes from a petrol tanker should be earthed **before** being used.

D

▷ **Conduction in solids**

In any solid conductor (e.g. a copper wire), an electric current is a flow of electrons.

H

A metal is a **good** conductor, because some of the electrons from the atoms can move freely and easily through the metal structure.

Answers:

1. negative   2. charged   3. negative   4. negative   5. negatively, positively

▷ Using electrostatics

An **electrostatic precipitator** can be used
to remove smoke particles in a chimney:

In the diagram, the smoke particles pick up
a positive charge as they pass by the grid (+).

They are then repelled by the positive grid
and attracted to the (negative) plates.
The particles stick there, until they are knocked
off and collected.

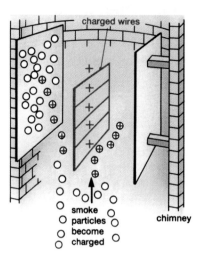

In a **photocopier**, a metal drum is charged up.
An image of the page to be copied is projected on to the drum. Where the
light shines on the drum the charges leak away, leaving a pattern of the page.

Black ink powder is attracted to these charged parts of the drum.
This ink is then transferred to a sheet of paper.
The paper is heated so that the ink powder melts and sticks to the paper.

▷ Conduction in liquids

Some liquids (called *electrolytes*) contain
charges (*ions*) which can move freely.
They are either ions dissolved in water
(e.g. salt solution) or melted ionic
compounds (e.g. molten sodium chloride).

A current flows because the **+** ions move
to the negative electrode, and the **–** ions
move to the positive electrode.

Uncharged substances are released at the
electrodes.
This is **electrolysis**.

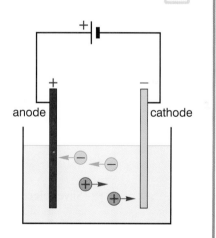

H

In electrolysis, the *mass* (or volume) of the
substance deposited or released at an electrode
increases in proportion to:
- the *current*,
- the *time* for which it flows.

Take care:

- Make sure you
  know about
  one use and
  one danger of
  electrostatics.

- Be clear about the different
  ways a current flows in a
  metal and in an electrolyte.

More details in **Physics for You**,
pages 247–253, 277–279.

Examination Questions – Static electricity

Module Test Questions

D 1 A polythene rod is rubbed with a dry cloth. The rod is then held close to a small electrically-charged bead hanging from a string. The diagram shows what happens to the bead.

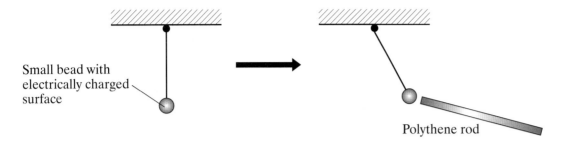

Match words from the list with the numbers **1–4** in the sentences.

discharged

electrons

negatively charged

positively charged

When the rod is rubbed ...... **1**....... are rubbed off the cloth on to the rod.

The surface of the rod is now ...... **2**...... .

The charged rod now attracts the bead because the surface of the bead is ....**3**...... .

If the bead is touched it is no longer attracted to the rod because the bead has been ...... **4**....... .

D 2 The diagram shows a metal
H spoon being silver plated.

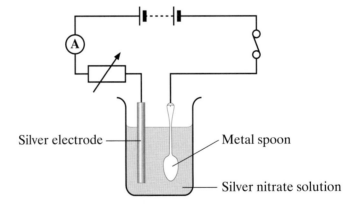

Silver electrode — Metal spoon

— Silver nitrate solution

Which **two** statements, **P, Q, R, S** or **T**, are correct?

   P   when the current is doubled, the amount of silver deposited is halved

   Q   when the time is doubled, the amount of silver deposited is four times as
         great

   R   when both current <u>and</u> time are doubled, the amount of silver deposited is
         four times as great

   S   when the current is doubled <u>and</u> the time is halved, the amount of silver
         deposited is halved

   T   when the current is four times as great <u>and</u> the time is halved,
         the amount of silver deposited is doubled

6

marks

Terminal Paper Questions

1 (a) The diagram shows an electrostatic precipitator in a chimney. This can be used to remove smoke particles from gases passing through the chimney.

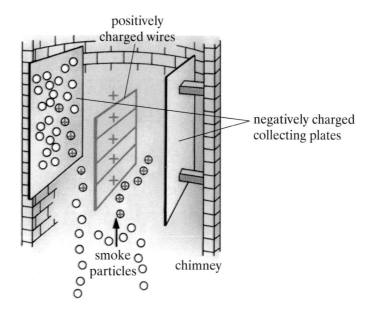

positively
charged wires

negatively charged
collecting plates

smoke
particles   chimney

Explain what happens to the smoke particles as they pass through the electrostatic precipitator.

....

....

....

....

....

....

....

....

....

(5 marks)

(b) Name another device that makes use of electrostatic attraction.

....

(1 mark)

(c) Explain why pipes from petrol tankers should be earthed before being used.

....

....

....

....

....

(3 marks)

9
marks

Answers on page 111

8 **Mains** electricity

---

1. Mains electricity in the UK is supplied at a . . . . voltage.
   If not used carefully, it can be . . . .
2. In a fuse, the wire should . . . . if the current is too . . . .

3. A mains plug has . . . . pins.
   Some parts of the plug are made of plastic, because plastic is a good . . . .
   Some parts are made of brass, because brass is a good . . . .

▷ The 3-pin plug

When connecting the wires you must ensure that:

- the blue wire is connected to the neutral terminal,
- the brown wire is connected to the live terminal,
- the green/yellow wire is connected to the earth terminal,
- the cable should be held firmly in the cable-grip,
- a *fuse* of the correct value (rating) must be fitted.

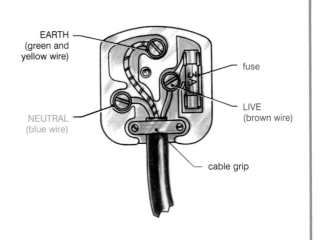

▷ The earth wire – for safety

In the UK, the mains supply is 230 V and can easily kill you.
Appliances with metal cases need to be **earthed**.
The case is connected to the earth pin (by the green/yellow wire).
If a fault connects the case to the live wire, then a large current flows to earth and melts the fuse.

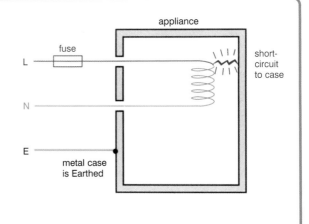

The **fuse**:

- must be in the live wire, so the appliance becomes disconnected,
- should have a value (rating) higher than (but as close as possible to) the normal working current,
- can be replaced by a circuit-breaker (see Topic 6).

▷ Alternating current (a.c.)

An alternating current (a.c.) is constantly changing direction, to and fro:

Compare this with direct current (d.c.) from a battery.

Mains electricity is an a.c. supply. In the UK it has a frequency of 50 hertz (50 Hz), so each cycle lasts for 1/50 second, as shown:

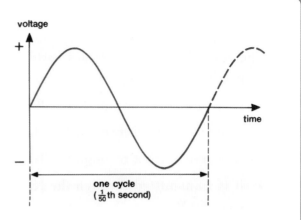

H

The mains supply in the UK is 230 volts.

The **live** terminal of the mains supply alternates between a positive and a negative voltage with respect to the neutral terminal, as shown above.

The **neutral** terminal stays at a voltage close to zero with respect to earth.

Take care:

Make sure you know how to wire a 3-pin mains plug.

▷ Measuring with an oscilloscope

An oscilloscope (CRO) displays a waveform.

It can be used to measure:
- the voltage (p.d.) of d.c. or a.c. supplies,
- the frequency of an a.c. supply.

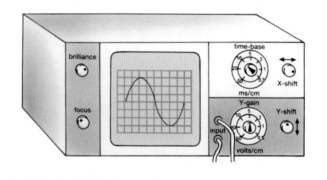

Example 1

A **d.c.** supply is connected to an oscilloscope:

before   *after*

Suppose the Y-sensitivity is 4 V/cm

You can see that the spot has moved up 2 squares = 2 cm

So:
the voltage = 2 cm × 4 V/cm
= <u>8 V</u>

Example 2

An a.c. supply is connected to a CRO with the time-base on:

before   *after*

Suppose the Y-sensitivity is 4 V/cm

The spot has moved up 2 cm

So:
Peak voltage = 2 cm × 4 V/cm
= <u>8 V</u>

Example 3

An a.c. supply is connected to an oscilloscope with the time-base on:

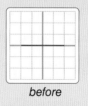 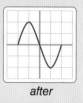

before   *after*

X-time-base = 0.01 seconds/cm

One complete oscillation = 4 cm
(horizontally)

So:
Time period = 4 cm × 0.01 s/cm
= <u>0.04 seconds</u>

Frequency = $\frac{1}{\text{time}} = \frac{1}{0.04} = 25\,\text{Hz}$

More details in **Physics for You**, pages 274–275, 305, 317.

Examination Questions – Mains electricity

Module Test Questions

1 Most homes in the UK have a mains electricity supply.

Which **two** of the following statements about mains electricity are true?

    A **it is supplied to homes at 230 volts**

    B **it is transmitted through the National Grid at 230 volts**

    C **it is transmitted through the National Grid with a frequency of 50 Hz**

    D **it is transmitted through the National Grid at a much higher frequency than 50 Hz**

    E **it is supplied to homes with a frequency of 230 Hz**

2 A family bought a second-hand DVD player. The current taken by the player is 1 A. When they checked the plug they found the faults labelled **1–4** on the diagram.

Match the words from the list with each of the labels **1–4**.

cable is loose

DVD player is not earthed

live wire is incorrectly connected

wrong fuse is used

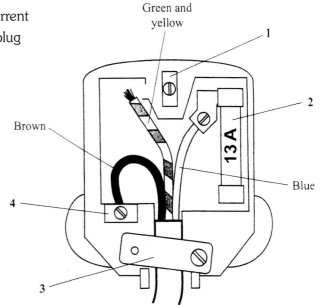

3 This question is about safety features for electrical appliances.

3.1 Electric cables have a plastic outer coat, and plastic covering each of the copper wires.

What is the most important reason for using plastic?

    A It is a better conductor than rubber.

    B It is flexible and so can be bent easily.

    C It prevents the current-carrying wires touching each other or other conductors.

    D It weighs little and so is a good choice when two layers of insulation are used.

3.2 An electric plug usually has three wires, two of which carry current to and from the appliance.

What is the purpose of the third wire?

    A It carries surplus current to and from the appliance when the live wire is overloaded.

    B It connects the neutral wire to earth so that it is always at 0 volts.

    C It protects the appliance from too large a current by melting.

    D It provides a path to earth for the current should the live wire touch the metal appliance case.

8 marks

Terminal Paper Questions

1 (a) Explain why mains appliances with metal cases need to be earthed.

....

....

....

....

....

....

(3 marks)

(b) State and explain which wire in a circuit should contain the fuse.

....

....

....

....

(2 marks)

(c) The value (rating) of the fuse in an appliance should be slightly higher than the normal working current.

  (i) Why should the value be higher?

....

....

....

(1 mark)

  (ii) Why should the value be only **slightly** higher?

....

....

....

(1 mark)

(d) Why is a circuit-breaker better than a fuse?

....

....

....

(1 mark)

8
marks

Answers on page 111

ELECTRO-MAGNETIC INDUCTION

▷ **ThinkAbout:**

1. Electricity is generated in . . . . stations, using energy from renewable or . . . . resources.

2. The electricity is supplied as . . . . current. This is distributed round the country using the . . . . Grid.

▷ **Producing electricity**

If a magnet is moved into this coil of wire, a current is produced ('induced') in the coil circuit.
It is converting kinetic energy to electrical energy.

If the other pole of the magnet is moved into the coil, the direction of the current is reversed.
If the magnet is moved out of the coil, the current is reversed.

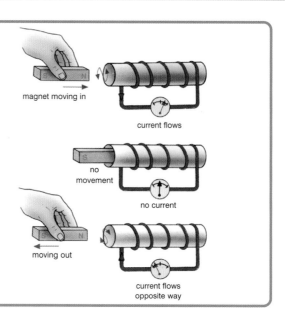

▷ **An a.c. generator** (or 'alternator' or 'dynamo')

A generator consists of a coil rotating in a magnetic field (or a magnet rotating in a coil):

When the wires of the coil 'cut through' the magnetic field lines, a voltage (p.d.) is produced between the ends of the wire.

This induced voltage can be increased by:
● using a coil with more turns,
● using a stronger magnet,
● rotating the coil faster,
● using a coil with a larger area.

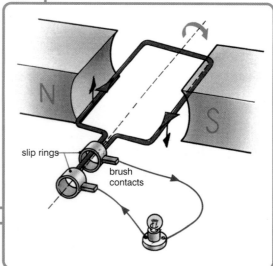

H In the diagram, the rotating coil cuts the magnetic field, inducing a current in the circuit. The slip-rings and brushes are used to connect the coil to the lamp while the coil is turning.

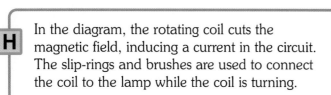

Answers: 1. power, non-renewable 2. alternating, national

▷ Transformers

Transformers are used to change the voltage of an a.c. supply. They do not work with d.c. They are used in the National Grid (see below).

D **H**

A transformer consists of 2 separate coils, wound on an iron core:

When an alternating voltage is applied across the primary coil, it produces a changing magnetic field.
This changing magnetic field induces an alternating voltage across the secondary coil.

The voltages are connected by:

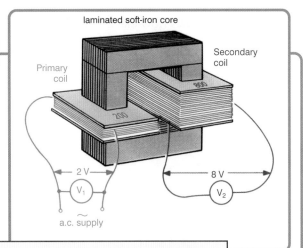

laminated soft-iron core

Primary coil

Secondary coil

2 V — V_1

8 V — V_2

a.c. supply

$$\frac{\text{voltage across primary}}{\text{voltage across secondary}} = \frac{\text{number of turns on primary}}{\text{number of turns on secondary}}$$

Example

A transformer has a primary coil with 200 turns, and a secondary coil with 800 turns (a 'step-up' transformer).
If the primary voltage is 2 V (a.c.), what is the secondary voltage?

Substituting the numbers in the equation shown above,

$$\frac{2\text{ V}}{\text{voltage across secondary}} = \frac{200}{800}$$

So: $\quad \dfrac{\text{voltage across secondary}}{2\text{ V}} = \dfrac{800}{200} \quad$ (by inverting both sides)

∴ $\quad$ voltage across secondary $= \dfrac{800}{200} \times 2\text{ V} \; = \underline{8\text{ V}}$ (a.c.)

▷ The National Grid

At power stations, transformers are used to produce very high voltages, before the electricity is distributed by power lines (the National Grid).
Local transformers reduce the voltage to safer levels for homes.

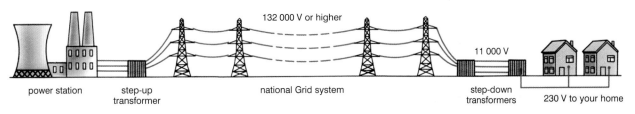

132 000 V or higher

11 000 V

power station   step-up transformer   national Grid system   step-down transformers   230 V to your home

The higher the voltage, the smaller the current needed to transfer energy at the same rate. So less energy is wasted by heating up the power lines.

H

More details in *Physics for You*, pages 302–309.

Take care:

Remember that a voltage is only induced when something moves or changes (a wire or a magnetic field).

Examination Questions – Electromagnetic induction

Module Test Questions

1 The diagram shows how electricity from power stations reaches our homes.

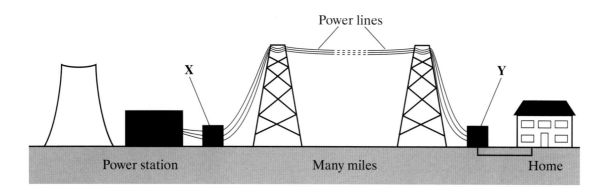

The voltage of the electricity is changed at points **X** and **Y**.

1.1 What is used to change the voltage?

    A A circuit breaker

    B A generator

    C A motor

    D A transformer

1.2 Which of the following statements is correct?

    A The voltage is increased at both **X** and **Y**

    B The voltage is increased at **X** and decreased at **Y**

    C The voltage is decreased at **X** and increased at **Y**

    D The voltage is decreased at both **X** and **Y**

1.3 The electric current used in **X** and **Y**…

    A must be d.c.

    B can be either a.c. or d.c.

    C must be a.c.

    D must be d.c. at **X** and a.c. at **Y**.

1.4 The power lines used to transmit electricity are called …

    A the National Grid.

    B nPower.

    C Powergen.

    D the World Wide Web.

———
4
marks

Terminal Paper Questions

1 • Diagram **1** shows a magnet being moved into a coil.

   • Diagram **2** shows a magnet stationary in the coil.

   • Diagram **3** shows a magnet being moved out of the coil.

The meter looks like this when no current is flowing.

(a) The position of the meter pointer has been drawn on diagram **1**.
    Draw the positions of the meter pointer on diagrams **2** and **3**.

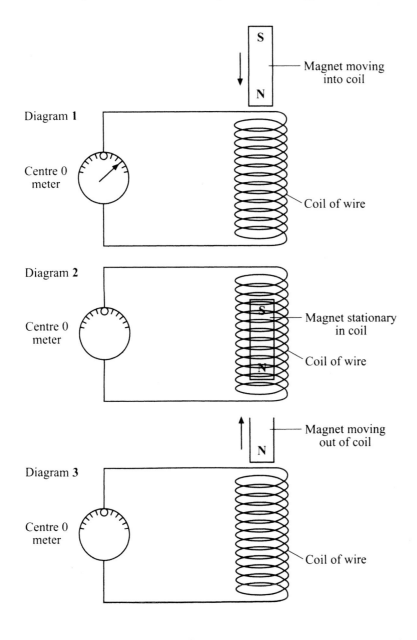

(2 marks)

(b) Bicycle dynamos generate electricity by rotating a magnet inside a coil of wire.

Give **two** ways of increasing the voltage produced by this kind of generator.

1. ....

2. ....

(2 marks)

4
marks

Answers on page 112

Getting the Grades – Electricity

Try this question, then compare your answer with the two examples opposite ▶

1   (a) The diagram shows a simple generator. The trace on the oscilloscope shows that the generator produces an alternating current.

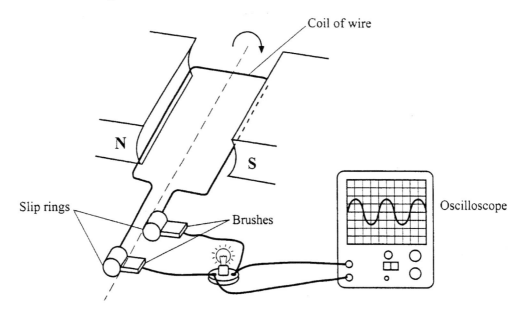

    (i) Explain how the generator works. Include in your answer the reasons why the slip rings and brushes are needed.

        ....

        ....

        ....

        ....

        .... *(4 marks)*

    (ii) What should be done to make the generator give the oscilloscope trace drawn below? Assume the controls on the oscilloscope are unchanged.

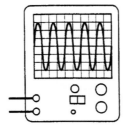

        ....

        ....

        .... *(2 marks)*

    (b) Explain why electricity is transmitted through the National Grid as alternating current (a.c.) rather than direct current (d.c.).

        ....

        ....

        .... *(3 marks)*

GRADE 'A' ANSWER

Ayesha has explained how the generator works and has used scientific terms correctly. To gain the final mark she should have explained that the brushes connect the slip rings to the circuit.

Ayesha gains both marks here as she says how much faster the coil must rotate.

Ayesha

1 (a) (i) The coil rotates and cuts through the magnetic field from the magnets. ✓
A voltage is induced across the coil. ✓
The slip rings let the coil rotate without getting tangled up. ✓

(ii) Rotate the coil twice as fast in the magnetic field. ✓✓

(b) Transformers do not work with dc. ✓
Transformers are used so there is less power loss in the lines. ✓ The voltage is stepped down before transmission across the National Grid ✗

Ayesha made an error here. The voltage is stepped up before transmission, not down.

7 marks = Grade A answer

▶ **Improve your Grades A up to A***
To get an A* you must give complete explanations to all parts of the question. Read through your answers to avoid silly mistakes.

GRADE 'C' ANSWER

*Joseph understands that the coil moves round in a magnetic field but uses scientific terms incorrectly. He should have said that a voltage is induced **across** the coil. He does not mention the brushes and slip rings in his answer even though he is told to in the question, so he cannot gain all the marks.*

Joseph

1 (a) (i) The coil moves round in the magnetic field from the magnets. ✓
There is a voltage induced through the coil. ✗

(ii) Turn the coil faster. ✓

(b) Because transformers only work with ac ✓ and transformers are used to step the voltage up in the power lines. ✓

Joseph's answer is incomplete. He does not say how much faster the coil turns, so he only gets 1 mark.

*Again the answer is incomplete. To get the final mark Joseph should explain **why** the voltage is stepped up.*

4 marks = Grade C answer

▶ **Improve your Grades C up to B**
Learn the work thoroughly and give complete answers to questions. Remember that each mark usually corresponds to a separate point in the answer. Take care to use scientific terms correctly.

10

VELOCITY and ACCELERATION

D

ThinkAbout:

1. What unit is speed measured in?
2. If a car accelerates, then its velocity is . . . .
3. A man runs 100 m in 20 seconds. What is his average speed?
4. "A car travels at 20 m/s." "A bus travels North at 20 m/s." Which of these is referring to a) speed, b) velocity?
5. Give a word for negative acceleration.

D

▷ Calculating speed

$$\text{average speed} \ (\text{in m/s}) = \frac{\text{distance travelled} \ (\text{in metres, m})}{\text{time taken} \ (\text{in seconds, s})}$$

D

▷ **Distance–time graphs** for a car:

A horizontal line means that the car is **at rest:** (not moving, stationary).

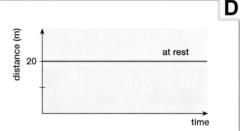

The car is now moving **at constant speed**, as shown by the distance increasing along a straight line:

If the car travels faster, the line will be steeper.

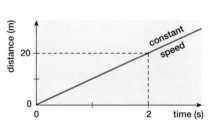

H

You can calculate the speed from the **gradient** or **slope** of the graph.

For the graph shown above,

$$\text{speed} = \frac{\text{distance travelled}}{\text{time taken}}$$

$$= \frac{20 \text{ m}}{2 \text{ s}}$$

$$= \underline{10 \text{ m/s}}$$

Example
Describe the motion of this cyclist:

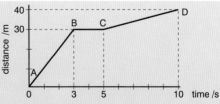

At first (A–B) he travels quite fast for 3 seconds.
After 30m, he stops (B–C) for 2 seconds.
Then he travels 10 m more slowly (C–D) for 5 s.

H Speed during A–B = 30/3 = 10 m/s
Speed during B–C = zero
Speed during C–D = 10/5 = 2 m/s

Velocity is speed in a particular direction.
For example, the pilot of a plane might be told to fly at 100 m/s due North. The direction is important.

If an object changes its velocity, it is **accelerating**.

▷ **Calculating acceleration**

$$\text{acceleration} \atop \text{(in m/s}^2\text{)} = \frac{\text{change in velocity (m/s)}}{\text{time taken for the change (s)}}$$

▷ **Velocity–time graphs** for a car:

A horizontal line means that the car is travelling with a **constant velocity**.

In this graph the car starts off from rest (velocity = zero) and **accelerates uniformly** in a straight line.

In this graph the car accelerates more rapidly. The graph has a steeper slope.

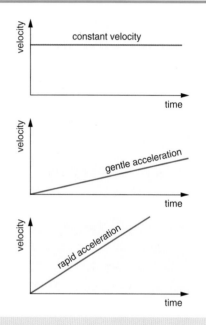

You can calculate the **acceleration** from the **gradient** or **slope** of the velocity–time graph.

In the graph shown at the right, the acceleration during P–Q

$$= \frac{\text{change in velocity}}{\text{time taken for change}}$$

$$= \frac{10 - 0 \text{ (m/s)}}{4 \text{ s}}$$

$$= \underline{2.5 \text{ m/s}^2}$$

The **distance travelled** is shown by the **area under** the velocity–time graph.

In the graph shown at the right, the distance travelled during P–Q

$$= \text{area of triangle under P–Q}$$
$$= \tfrac{1}{2} \times \text{base} \times \text{height}$$
$$= \tfrac{1}{2} \times 4 \times 10$$
$$= \underline{20 \text{ m}}$$

Example
Describe the motion of this car.

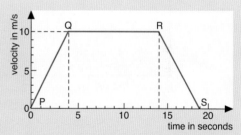

P–Q The car starts from rest and accelerates uniformly, until it reaches a velocity of 10 m/s after 4 s.

Q–R It stays at this speed for 10 seconds.

R–S The car decelerates, from 10 m/s to rest, in 5 s.

Take care:

• Make sure you look carefully in exam questions so you don't mix up distance–time and velocity–time graphs.

• In calculations make sure you show your working ... and include the correct units.

More in *Physics for You*, pages 130–134.

Examination Questions – Velocity and acceleration

Terminal Paper Questions

D 1 The table gives values of distance and time for a car travelling along a road.

Distance in metres	0	20	40	60	80	100
Time in seconds	0	1	2	3	4	5

(a) Draw a graph of distance against time.
    Two of the points have been plotted for you.

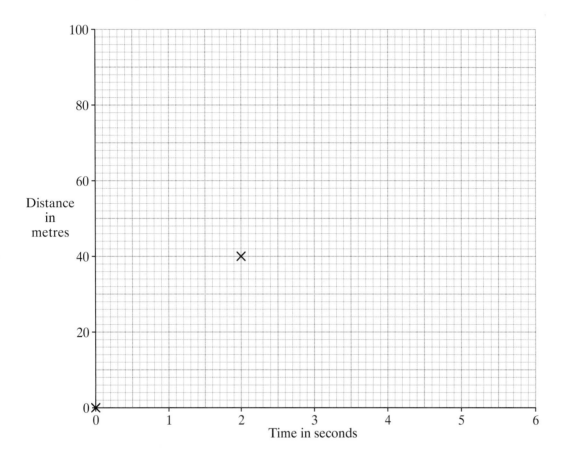

(3 marks)

(b) Use your graph to find:

   (i) the distance travelled in 2.5 seconds;

                                             Distance = ... metres

   (ii) the time at which the distance is 30 metres.

                                             Time = ... seconds

(2 marks)

(c) Complete the sentence by crossing out the **two** lines which are wrong.

The car is	slowing down
	moving at a steady speed
	speeding up

(1 mark)

6
marks

2 A car travels on a long straight road.

The graph shows how the speed of the car changes with time.

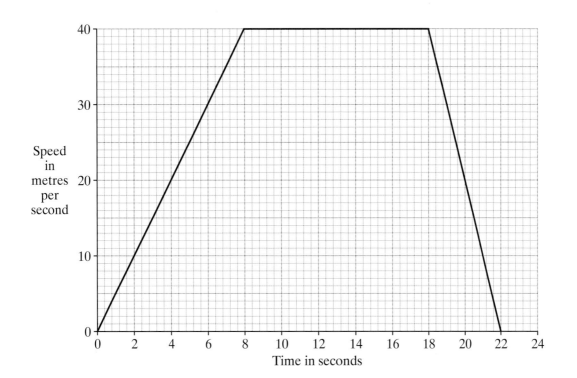

(a) Calculate the acceleration of the car during the first 8 seconds.
   Show clearly how you work out your final answer and give the unit.

   ....

   ....

   ....

   ....

                              Acceleration = ...

                                                              (4 marks)

(b) Calculate the distance travelled, in metres, between 18 and 22 seconds.
   Show clearly how you work out your final answer.

   ....

   ....

   ....

   ....

                              Distance = ... m

                                                              (3 marks)

Answers on page 112

11

ThinkAbout:

1. Cars and bicycles slow down because of the force of . . . . The brakes get . . . .
2. The force of friction always acts in the . . . . direction to the movement.
3. If the forces on an object cancel out they are said to be . . . .
   If they are not balanced then there is a . . . . force.

Balanced forces

If the forces on an object are balanced (no resultant force) then:

- if it is at rest, it stays at rest,
- if it is moving, it keeps on moving at a constant speed in a straight line.

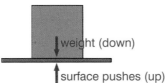

Object on a table
The forces are balanced

Car travelling at constant velocity
The forces are balanced

D

Unbalanced forces : resultant force

If the forces on an object do not cancel out, an unbalanced (resultant) force acts on the object, so that:

- a stationary object will start to move in the direction of the resultant force,
- an object already moving in the direction of the force will speed up (accelerate),
- an object moving in the opposite direction to the force will slow down (decelerate).

The car is accelerating
There is an unbalanced (resultant) force

The greater the resultant force, the greater the acceleration (or deceleration).
The bigger the mass of the object, the bigger the force needed to give it the same acceleration.

D

Friction

A force of friction acts:

- when an object moves through air or water,
- when solid surfaces slide, or try to slide, across each other.

The objects heat up (and wear away).

Gravity

Falling objects are accelerated downwards by gravity.
On Earth, the gravitational field strength is about 10 N/kg.
Weight is the pull of gravity on an object:

weight	=	**mass**	×	**gravitational field strength**
(newton, N)		(kilogram, kg)		(newton/kilogram, N/kg)

Example

What is the weight (on Earth) of a mass of 3 kg?

Weight = mass × gravitational field strength
= 3 kg × 10 N/kg
= <u>30 newtons</u>   (30 N)

▷ Stopping distance

D

The total stopping distance of a car depends on:

- The 'thinking distance'. This depends on the driver's reaction time (which depends on tiredness, drugs and alcohol).
- The 'braking distance'. This depends on the weather conditions (e.g. wet/icy roads) and the vehicle (e.g. worn brakes/tyres).

The greater the speed of the car, the more braking force, or distance, needed to stop it.

▷ Terminal velocity

D

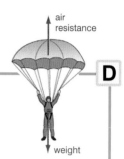

When an object falls through a fluid (gas or liquid), the faster it moves, the greater the force of friction.

When a body falls:
- at the start, it accelerates (due to the force of gravity (weight),
- frictional forces (e.g. air resistance) increase ...until they balance the gravitational force,
- then the resultant force is zero, and the body falls at its 'terminal' velocity.

▷ Force and acceleration

D H

One newton (1 N) is the **force** needed to give a mass of one kilogram (1 kg) an acceleration of one metre per second squared (1 m/s²).

force	=	mass	×	acceleration
(newton, N)		(kilogram, kg)		(metre/second squared, m/s²)

Example

What is the force needed to give a mass of 3 kg an acceleration of 2 m/s²?

force = mass × acceleration

= 3 kg × 2 m/s²

= <u>6 newtons</u>   (6 N)

To see how to calculate an acceleration, see Topic 10.

Take care:

- Don't confuse mass (in kg) with weight (in N).

- Weight is a force (in N) and always acts downwards. Friction is a force (in N) and always acts backwards (opposing the movement).

- Remember an unbalanced force always produces an acceleration.

- In calculations, show your working and make sure that you use the right units.

More details in **Physics for You**, pages 73, 75–77, 92–99, 136, 138–139.

Examination Questions – Forces

Terminal Paper Questions

D **1** Four of the forces that act on this container ship are shown in the diagram as **A**, **B**, **C** and **D**.

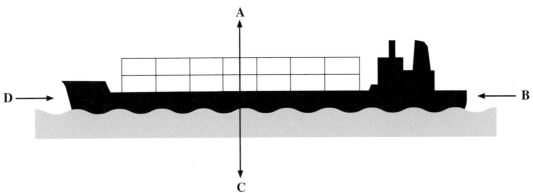

Complete each sentence by choosing the correct letters, **A**, **B**, **C** or **D**.
The first one has been done for you.

At the start, the ship is not moving because forces **B** and **D** are balanced.

The ship begins to move forward when forces .... and .... are unbalanced.

When the ship is moving at a steady speed, forces .... and .... are balanced.

The ship stops at a port. All of the containers are taken off and this changes force ....

(3 marks)

$\dfrac{}{3}$ marks

D **2** The diagrams below show the total stopping distance of a motorcyclist travelling at different speeds.

At 13 m/s (30 mph)

Thinking   **Braking**   Overall stopping
distance 9 m   distance 14 m   distance 23 m

At 22 m/s (50 mph)

Thinking   **Braking**   Overall stopping
distance 15 m   distance 38 m   distance 53 m

At 31 m/s (70 mph)

Thinking   **Braking**   Overall stopping
distance 21 m   distance 75 m   distance 96 m

(a) Describe how the thinking distance and the braking distance change with the speed of the motorcyclist.

....

....

....

....

(2 marks)

(b) (i) Name **two** factors, other than speed of the motorcycle, which would increase the thinking distance of the motorcyclist.

1 ....

....

2 ....

....

(2 marks)

(ii) Name **two** factors which would increase the braking distance of the motorcyclist on a wet road.

1 ....

....

2 ....

....

(2 marks)

6 marks

D
H
3 The diagram shows a person pushing a supermarket trolley, and the forces acting on the trolley.

(a) The mass of the trolley is 20 kg.

The resultant forward Force, **F$_R$**, is 5 N.

Calculate the acceleration of the trolley.

....

....

....

Acceleration = ... m/s^2

(3 marks)

(b) The trolley starts from rest.

Calculate the speed of the trolley after 8 seconds.

....

....

....

Speed = ... m/s

(3 marks)

6 marks

12 Work and energy

▷ **ThinkAbout:**

1. A moving object has movement energy, also called . . . . energy.
2. When an object is lifted to a higher place, it is given . . . . potential . . . .
3. Energy can be . . . . from one form to . . . .
4. A falling object is . . . . energy from . . . . potential energy to . . . . energy.
5. A stretched catapult has . . . . potential . . . .

D

▷ **Work and energy**

When a force moves an object, energy is transferred and work is done. In fact:

work done	=	energy transferred
(joules, J)		(joules, J)

To calculate the work done (energy transferred):

work done	**=**	**force applied**	**×**	**distance moved in the direction of the force**
(joules, J)		(newtons, N)		(metres, m)

Example 1

How much energy is transferred if a force of 2 N moves through a distance of 10 m?

work done = force × distance moved
          = 2 N × 10 m
          = 20 joules (20 J)

∴ energy transferred = work done = 20 J

▷ **Gravitational potential energy**

When an object is lifted up, work is done against the force of gravity, its weight.

It follows (from the equations above) that:

H

change in gravitational potential energy	**=**	**weight**	**×**	**change in vertical height**
(joules, J)		(newtons, N)		(metres, m)

Example 2

A man lifts up a brick of mass 5 kg from the floor to a shelf 2 metres high.
What is the change in gravitational potential energy of the brick?

Step 1 : Find the weight first (see Topic 11).

    weight = mass × gravitational field strength
             = 5 kg × 10 N/kg   = 50 N

Step 2 :
change in gravitational potential energy = weight × change in vertical height

             = 50 N × 2 m   = 100 joules

Answers:
1. kinetic   2. gravitational, energy   3. transferred/transformed/changed, another
4. transferring, gravitational, kinetic   5. elastic, energy

▷ Potential energy

Gravitational potential energy is the energy *stored* in an object because of the height it has been lifted to, against the force of gravity.

Elastic potential energy is the energy stored in an elastic object, when work has been done on the object to change its shape (eg. a catapult).

D **H**

▷ Kinetic energy

An object has more kinetic energy:
- the greater its mass, and
- the greater its speed.

In fact:

kinetic energy	=	$\frac{1}{2}$	×	**mass**	×	**speed²**
(joules, J)				(kilogram, kg)		(m/s)²

Example 3

A car of mass 800 kg is travelling at 10 m/s. How much work must be done to stop it?

kinetic energy $= \frac{1}{2} \times$ mass $\times$ speed²

$= \frac{1}{2} \times 800 \text{ kg} \times (10 \text{ m/s})^2$

$= \frac{1}{2} \times 800 \text{ kg} \times 100 \text{ m}^2/\text{s}^2$

$= 40\,000$ joules   (40 kJ)

To stop the car,
work done = energy transferred = 40 kJ
This energy will be transferred to heat in the brakes/tyres.

10 m/s

mass = 800 kg

braking force

D

▷ Power (*see also* Topic 2)

Power is measured in watts (W).   1000 W = 1 kW

power (watts, W)	=	$\dfrac{\textbf{energy transferred (J)}}{\textbf{time taken (s)}}$	=	$\dfrac{\textbf{work done (J)}}{\textbf{time taken (s)}}$

Example 4

A motorbike engine exerts a force of 1000 N for a distance of 200 m, taking 10 seconds. What is the power of the engine?

Step 1 :
work done = force × distance moved   (see opposite page)

$= 1000 \text{ N} \times 200 \text{ m}$

$= 200\,000$ joules

Step 2 :

power $= \dfrac{\text{work done}}{\text{time taken}} = \dfrac{200\,000 \text{ J}}{10 \text{ s}} = 20\,000 \text{ W}$ (20 kW)

Take care:

- Remember work done against frictional forces is transferred mainly as heat.

- In calculations, always show your working ... so you may then get some marks even if the final answer is wrong.

More details in **Physics for You**, pages 107–109, 116–119.

Examination Questions – Work and energy

Terminal Paper Questions

D 1 The diagram shows a person pushing a crate up a slope on to a lorry.

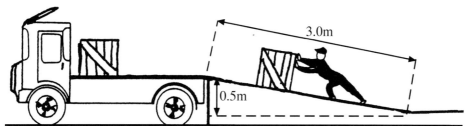

(a) The person pushes the crate along the slope with a force of 200 N.

Calculate the work done pushing the crate along the slope.

Write down the equation you are going to use.

....

(1 mark)

Show clearly how you work out your final answer.

....

....

....

....

Work done = ... J

(2 marks)

(b) The mass of the crate is 60 kg.

(i) Calculate the approximate weight of the crate.

Show clearly how you work out your final answer.

....

....

....

....

Weight = ... N

(2 marks)

(ii) Explain why more energy is transferred by pushing the crate along the slope than by lifting the crate the vertical distance 0.5 m.

....

....

....

(2 marks)

7
marks

2 The pictures show a 'wrecking ball' used to demolish buildings. The ball swings on the end of a long cable.

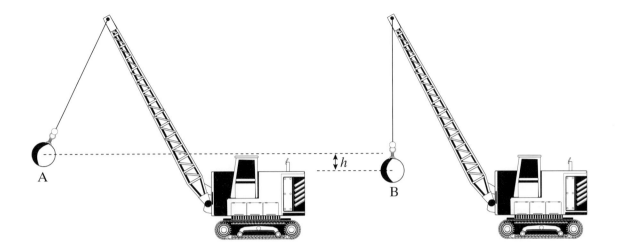

(a) As the ball swings from its position in A to its position in B it gains 225 000 J of kinetic energy. The mass of the ball is 2000 kg.

  (i) Write down the equation that links kinetic energy, mass and speed.

....

(1 mark)

  (ii) Calculate the speed of the ball as it passes through its position in B.

     Show clearly how you work out your final answer.

....

....

....

                                  Speed = ... m/s

(2 marks)

(b) As the ball swings from its position in A to its position in B it falls through the vertical height, *h*, shown on the diagram. Its change in gravitational potential energy is 225 000 J.

  (i) Write down the equation that links change in gravitational potential energy, weight and the height *h*.

....

(1 mark)

  (ii) Calculate the height *h*.

     Show clearly how you work out your final answer.

....

....

....

                       Height *h* = ... m

(2 marks)

6

marks

13 The Solar System

> ▶ **ThinkAbout:**
>
> 1. The Earth spins on its own axis once every . . . . (. . . . hours).
>   For the half which faces the Sun, it is . . . . ;
>   for the other half it is . . . .
> 2. The Earth orbits the Sun once each . . . . (. . . . days).
>
> 3. The planets move in . . . . around the . . . . We see the planets because they . . . . light from the . . . .
> 4. . . . . can be put in orbit round the Earth.
> 5. The patterns of stars in the night sky are called . . . .

▶ Gravitational force

The Earth, the Sun, the Moon and **all** other bodies **attract** each other, with a force called gravity.
The pull of gravity on you, by the Earth, is called your weight.

As the distance between 2 bodies increases, the force of gravity decreases.
At twice the distance it is only $\frac{1}{4}$ as much:

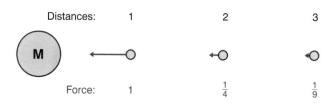

Distances: 1   2   3

Force: 1 $\frac{1}{4}$ $\frac{1}{9}$

▶ Orbits of planets and comets

The **planets** are held in orbit round the Sun, by the gravitational pull of the Sun.
Their orbits are slightly squashed circles (ellipses) with the Sun quite close to the centre.

To stay in orbit at a particular distance, a planet must move at a particular speed round the Sun.
The further away a planet is, the longer it takes to make a complete orbit (e.g. Pluto takes 248 years).

Comets are lumps of ice, dust and gas.
They are held in orbit by the gravitational pull of the Sun.
They have very elliptical orbits, so sometimes they are near the Sun and sometimes far out in the Solar System (often beyond Pluto).

When they are near the Sun they can sometimes be seen shining.

Saturn

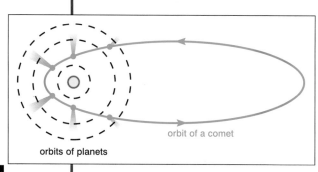

orbit of a comet

orbits of planets

▶ Satellites and gravity

Satellites can be launched to orbit the Earth.
They stay in orbit because of the combination of
the high speed and the force of gravity of the Earth.

To stay in a particular orbit, they have to travel at
the right speed.

The higher the satellite, the **slower** the speed and
the **longer** it takes for one orbit.

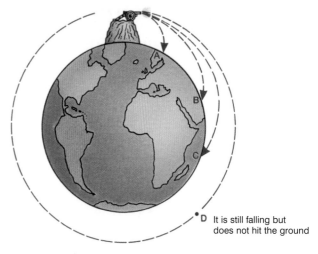

D It is still falling but
does not hit the ground

*Satellites must travel fast enough
for the orbit they are in*

▶ Uses of satellites

- Monitoring or observation satellites
  e.g. weather satellites, military (spy) satellites.
- Communications satellites
  e.g. for transmitting telephone calls and
  TV programmes.
- Astronomical satellites
  e.g. space telescopes taking photos outside
  the Earth's atmosphere.

▶ Satellite orbits

Satellites can be launched into **polar** orbit or
equatorial orbit.

polar orbit

equatorial orbit

Monitoring satellites are usually put into a low
polar orbit, so that as the Earth spins beneath
them they can scan different parts of the Earth.

Communication satellites are usually put into
a high equatorial orbit.

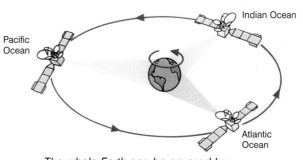

Indian Ocean

Pacific Ocean

Atlantic Ocean

*The whole Earth can be covered by
just three geostationary satellites*

The orbit is adjusted so that the satellite moves
round at *exactly the same rate* as the Earth
spins i.e. once *every 24 hours.*
This means that the satellite is always in the
same position when viewed from Earth.
This is a **geostationary** orbit.

There is space for only about 400 geostationary
satellites or they would interfere with each
other's signals.

More details in **Physics for You**,
pages 158–163, 168–169, 221, 320.

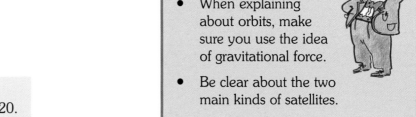

Take care:

- When explaining
  about orbits, make
  sure you use the idea
  of gravitational force.
- Be clear about the two
  main kinds of satellites.

Examination Questions – The Solar System

Terminal Paper Questions

1 The diagram shows two satellites going round the Earth.

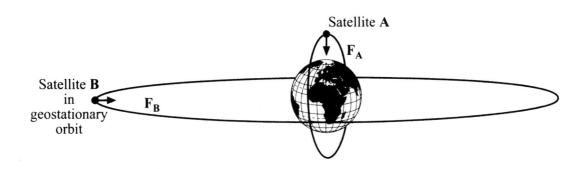

The two satellites have the same mass.

(a) Complete each of the sentences by crossing out the **two** lines in each box that are wrong.

(i) The satellites are attracted to the Earth by a force called

> air resistance
>
> friction
>
> gravity

(ii) Satellite **B** is further from the Earth than satellite **A**, so Force F_A is

> smaller than F_B
>
> the same size as F_B
>
> bigger than F_B

(iii) The time taken for one orbit by satellite **A** is

> less than the time for satellite **B**
>
> the same as the time for satellite **B**
>
> more than the time for satellite **B**

(3 marks)

(b) The orbits of communication satellites are described as *geostationary*.
Explain why.

To gain full marks in this question you should write your ideas in good English.
Put them into a sensible order and use the correct scientific words.

....

....

....

....

(2 marks)

5

marks

2 Complete the sentences by choosing the correct words from the box.

galaxies	magnetic	gravitational	circular
planet	star	elliptical	Sun

The Sun is a .... in the Solar System.

The planets are held in orbit around the Sun by the .... pull of the Sun.

Comets are lumps of ice, dust and gas. The shape of their orbits is ....
This means that they are much closer to the .... at some times than at others.

(4 marks)

4 marks

3 Communication satellites are put into a geostationary orbit above the Earth.

(a) How long does a satellite in a geostationary orbit take to orbit the Earth?

....

(1 mark)

(b) (i) Name another type of satellite and compare its orbit with that of a communications satellite.

....

....

....

....

(4 marks)

5 marks

Answers on page 114

14

Stars and the Universe

> **ThinkAbout:**
> 1. Our nearest star is the . . . .
> 2. A group of millions of stars, like the Milky Way, is called a . . . .
> 3. The Universe is thought to have started in the Big . . . .
>   This happened . . . . of years ago.

▶ **The birth of a star**

The Sun and other stars formed when enough dust and gas from space were pulled together by gravitational attraction.

At the same time, smaller masses can form and be attracted to orbit round the star, as planets.

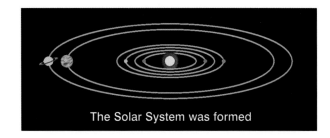

The Solar System was formed

▶ **The life and death of a star**

In a stable star like the Sun, 2 forces are balanced:
- the force of gravity (inwards) trying to crush the star,
- forces of expansion (outwards) due to the high temperature.

H

The energy of a star is produced by nuclear fusion (like a hydrogen bomb).
The nuclei of lighter elements (mainly hydrogen and helium) fuse together, to produce nuclei of heavier elements.

As a star gets older, it expands to become a red giant or a red supergiant, as shown:

H

A red supergiant may contract and then explode as a supernova.
This explosion causes heavy elements to form ... which later become the dust for making new stars and planets (and human beings).

Later the dying star contracts to form a dwarf star, or a neutron star, or a black hole. Its matter is extremely dense.

H

In extreme cases, the star is so dense, and the pull of gravity so strong, that nothing can escape from it, not even light. It is a black hole.
We can't see a black hole, but we may see its effect (e.g. X-rays emitted when matter spirals into it).

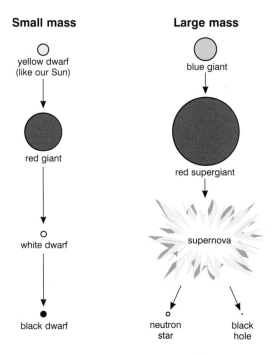

Small mass

yellow dwarf
(like our Sun)

red giant

white dwarf

black dwarf

Large mass

blue giant

red supergiant

supernova

neutron
star

black
hole

Answers: 1. Sun 2. galaxy 3. Bang; billions

▶ Galaxies

Our Sun is one of millions of stars in our Milky Way galaxy.
The Universe as a whole is made of at least a billion galaxies.

Within a galaxy the stars are often millions of times farther apart
than the planets in our Solar System.
And the galaxies are often million of times farther apart than the
stars within a galaxy.

H

▶ The red shift

Light coming to us from other galaxies is shifted
towards the red end of the spectrum.
The farther away a galaxy is, the bigger this 'red-shift'.

red shift

Scientists believe that this means:
- other galaxies are moving away from us, quickly,
- the farther away from us a galaxy is, the faster
  it is moving away from us.

This suggests that:
- the whole Universe is expanding (like the dots on
  a balloon move farther apart as the balloon
  expands),
- the Universe began billions of years ago with a
  huge expansion (the 'Big Bang').

▶ The search for life in the Universe

If there is, or has been, life on planets in our Solar System
or around other stars, then we may be able to find
evidence:

- *By looking for living organisms* (e.g. microbes) or
  their fossils on other planets, perhaps by using robots
  to collect samples.

- *By looking for the effects of living organisms*
  (e.g. the chemical changes they produce).
  For example, most of the oxygen on Earth is due to
  living organisms.

- *By listening with radio telescopes* for any radio
  signals from advanced civilisations like ours.
  This is the SETI project (**S**earch for **E**xtra-**T**errestrial
  Intelligence).

Take care:
- Be clear about
  the two main
  life-cycles of
  stars.

- Make sure you understand
  the evidence that leads
  scientists to believe in the
  Big Bang.

- Be clear about the three
  ways of searching for life
  elsewhere in the Universe.

More details in **Physics for You**,
pages 163–167.

Examination Questions – Stars and the Universe

Terminal Paper Questions

1 A space probe, Beagle 2, was launched in 2003 by the European Space Agency. It is part of the *Mars Express* programme.

The project leader Professor Colin Pillinger, commented: "Britain has a history of exploring our planet. It is about time we started exploring the other planets as well".

Space probes are designed to send pictures back to Earth, and collect samples of soil and rock.

(a) Complete the sentence by choosing the correct words from the box.

fossils	**hydrogen**	**iron**	**sulphur**	**water**

If scientists found .... or .... on Mars, it would indicate that there may be, or once was, life there.   *(2 marks)*

(b) The sending of probes deep into space is very expensive, and the space flights would take too long. For over forty years, a *SETI* team in the USA has been monitoring signals coming from space.

(i) What is *SETI*?

....

(1 mark)

(ii) What piece of equipment does a *SETI* team use?

....

(1 mark)

(iii) The graph shows radio noise, of various wavelengths, detected by a *SETI* team.

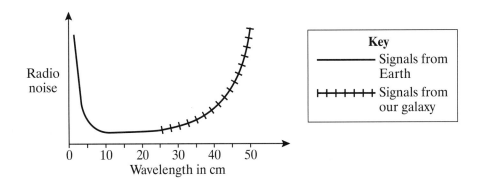

Choose a range of wavelengths from the box to complete the sentence.

0–5	**10–20**	**30–40**	**40–50**

To monitor signals coming from space, the *SETI* team would investigate radio

signals with wavelengths in the range .... cm.

(1 mark)

5 marks

2 When a star "dies", a *black hole* may be formed.

(a) Describe, as fully as you can, a *black hole*.

....

....

....

(3 marks)

H (b) *Black holes* cannot be seen.
How can they be detected?

....

....

....

....

(3 marks)

6
marks

H **3** The "big bang" theory is one theory of the origin of the Universe.

(a) Explain what is meant by the "big bang" theory.

....

....

....

....

(2 marks)

(b) One piece of evidence for the "big bang" theory is "red-shift".

(i) What is "red-shift"?

....

....

(1 mark)

(ii) Explain how "red-shift" leads to the "big bang" theory.

....

....

....

....

....

....

(4 marks)

7
marks

Answers on page 114

Getting the Grades – Forces

Try this question, then compare your answer with the two examples opposite ▶

D 1 A car travelling along a straight road has to stop and wait at red traffic lights. The graph shows how the velocity of the car changes after the traffic lights turn green.

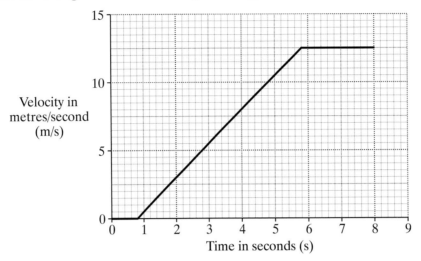

Velocity in metres/second (m/s) vs Time in seconds (s)

(a) Between the traffic lights changing to green and the car starting to move there is a time delay. This is called reaction time. Write down **one** factor that could affect the driver's reaction time.

.... *(1 mark)*

D H (b) Calculate the distance the car travels while accelerating. Show clearly how you work out your answer.

....

....

Distance = ... metres

(3 marks)

(c) Calculate the acceleration of the car. Show clearly how you work out your final answer and give units.

....

....

....

Acceleration = ...

(4 marks)

D H (d) The mass of the car is 900 kg.

(i) Write down the equation that links acceleration, force and mass.

.... *(1 mark)*

(ii) Calculate the force used to accelerate the car. Show clearly how you work out your final answer.

....

....

Force = ...

(2 marks)

GRADE 'A' ANSWER

Jack knows that being tired is one of the things that slows reaction time and so gets the first mark. He would have got the mark for other things too, such as the driver not concentrating or being under the influence of drugs or alcohol.

Jack knows that the area under a velocity-time graph gives the distance travelled. He reads the numbers correctly from the graph to find the area under the part of the graph where the car is accelerating. Unfortunately he makes a slip in the final part of the calculation. The correct answer is 31.25, but he loses only one mark as the rest of his working is correct.

Jack

1 (a) Being tired. ✓
(b) Distance travelled = area under graph ✓
Distance travelled = $\frac{1}{2}$ × (5.8 − 0.8) × 12.5 ✓
Distance travelled = $\frac{1}{2}$ × 5 × 12.5
Distance travelled = 30.25 metres ✗
(c) Acceleration = slope of graph ✓
Acceleration = (12.5 − 0)/(5.8 − 0.8) ✓
Acceleration = 12.5/5.0
Acceleration = 2.5 m/s ✓ ✗
(d) (i) force = mass × acceleration ✓
(ii) force = 900 × 2.5 ✓
force = 2250 newtons ✓

Jack knows that the slope of a velocity-time graph gives the acceleration. He reads the numbers from the graph and correctly works out the acceleration and so gains three marks. He loses the last mark because he forgets that the units of acceleration are m/s².

Jack gains all three marks for part (d) as he knows the equation and uses it to calculate the force correctly.

9 marks = Grade A answer

▶ Improve your Grades   A up to A*

Take care with calculations. Maximize your marks by showing all your working and if you have time go back and check calculations for errors. Make sure that you know the units for all the quantities that you use in physics and can write the symbols for them correctly.

GRADE 'C' ANSWER

Sophie knows that driving too fast increases the stopping distance of a car, but this is not an answer to the question asked, so she does not get the mark.

Sophie knows that the area under a velocity-time graph gives the distance travelled. The question asks for the distance the car travels while accelerating, which is the area under the sloping part of the graph. Sophie also finds the distance travelled while the car is going at a constant speed so she does not get the last two marks.

Sophie

1 (a) Driving too fast. ✗
(b) Distance travelled = area under graph ✓
Distance travelled = $\frac{1}{2}$ × (5.8 − 0.8) × 12.5
           + (2 × 12.5) ✗
Distance travelled = $\frac{1}{2}$ × 5 × 12.5 + 25
Distance travelled = 56.25 metres ✗
(c) Acceleration = slope of graph ✓
Acceleration = (5.8 − 0.8)/(12.5 − 0) ✓
Acceleration = 5.0/12.5
Acceleration = 0.4 ✗ ✗
(d) (i) newtons = kilograms × acceleration ✗
(ii) force= 900 × 0.4 ✓
force = 360 newtons ✓

Sophie knows that the slope of a velocity-time graph gives the acceleration. She reads the numbers from the graph correctly and so gets the second mark. Unfortunately Sophie puts the calculation upside down and forgets to give a unit so she loses the last two marks.

Sophie has used some units in her equation, instead of the quantities given in the question, so she does not get the mark.

Sophie's value for acceleration is wrong, but she uses it correctly with the mass to calculate the force and so gains both marks.

5 marks = Grade C answer

▶ Improve your Grades   C up to B

Always read the question carefully and make sure you answer what is asked. If you a taking values from graphs take care that you read the numbers correctly and that you are using the correct region on the graph. Know how to find slopes of graphs and areas under graphs. Learn word equations carefully and do not mix up quantities and units.

15

Waves Waves Waves

> ## ThinkAbout:
> 1. Light can be . . . . from a mirror.
>   The angle of incidence is . . . . to the angle of . . . .
> 2. Sound can be reflected. It is called an . . . .
> 3. When light (or sound) goes from one substance to another, the direction can . . . . This is called . . . .
> 4. Sound can also be . . . .

▷ Longitudinal waves

A sound wave is a longitudinal wave.
The vibrations are in the same direction as the wave is travelling:
Sound waves can travel through solids, liquids and gases.

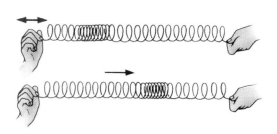

▷ Transverse waves

Water waves, waves on ropes, and light waves are transverse waves.
The vibrations are at right-angles to the direction the wave travels:
Light waves are transverse waves and can travel through a vacuum.

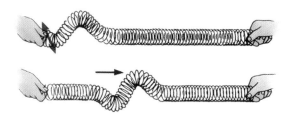

▷ Amplitude, wavelength, frequency

wavelength

wavelength

a is the **amplitude**.
The number of complete wavelengths (or vibrations) in each second is called the **frequency**, measured in hertz (Hz).

> **D**
>
> Waves transfer energy from one place to another.
> For any wave, without any matter being transferred:
>
> | **wave speed** | **=** | **frequency** | **×** | **wavelength** |
> | (m/s) | | (hertz, Hz) | | (metres, m) |
>
> *Example*
>
> A water wave has a wavelength of 3 m and a frequency of 2 Hz. What is its speed?
>
> wave speed = frequency × wavelength
> = 2 Hz × 3 m = 6 m/s

▷ Reflection

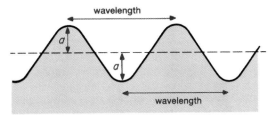

▷ Refraction

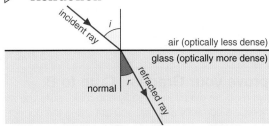

▷ Refraction

When light travels from glass to air,
it is refracted away from the normal:

This is because of the change in speed.
Light travels more slowly in glass, and
faster in air.

Some of the light is reflected at the boundary.

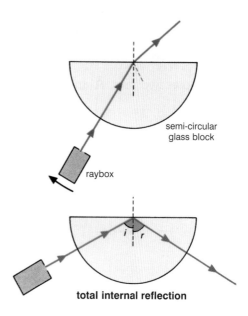

semi-circular
glass block

raybox

▷ Total internal reflection

If the angle of incidence is greater than the
critical angle, **all** of the light is reflected inside:
This is called total internal reflection.

total internal reflection

D

▷ Using total internal reflection

Light can travel down an optical fibre,
by repeated total internal reflection.

This can be used in telephone systems
and by doctors using endoscopes:

Other uses of total internal reflection
include reflecting prisms, bicycle
reflectors, and "cat's eye" reflectors.

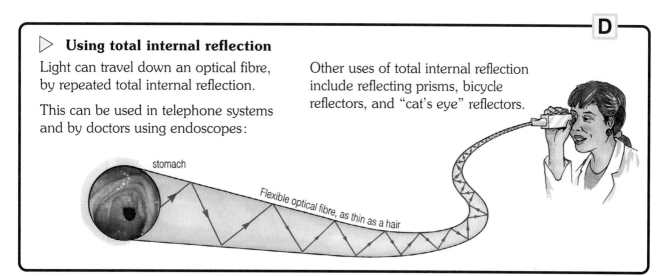

stomach

Flexible optical fibre, as thin as a hair

D

▷ Diffraction

When a wave moves through a gap, or
past an obstacle, it spreads out:
There is more diffraction with a smaller gap.

Electromagnetic radiation (including light)
and sound can be diffracted. This is
evidence that they are waves.

Because of diffraction:
* sounds can be heard in the shadow of
  buildings,
* radio signals can sometimes be
  received in the shadow of hills.

More details in **Physics for You**,
pages 174–178, 184–187, 192–197, 200.

Take care:

Don't confuse
'reflection',
'refraction' and
'diffraction'.

Terminal Paper Questions

1 The diagram shows two rays, **A** and **B**, entering a glass block from air. Both rays pass through the block.

Complete the diagram to show the direction taken by **each** ray:

- as it passes through the glass block;
- as it leaves the glass block.

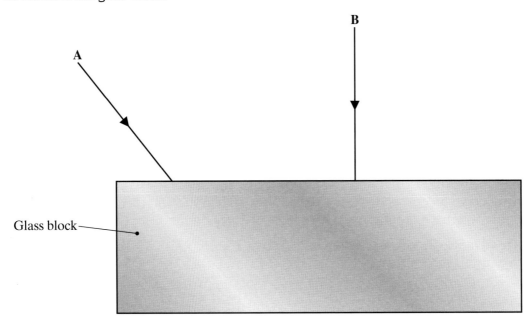

(3 marks)

3
marks

2 The diagram shows a transverse wave.

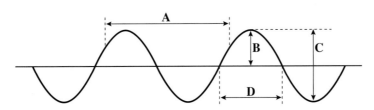

(a) Which of **A**, **B**, **C** or **D** is:

   (i) the wavelength;   ....

   (ii) the amplitude?   ....   *(2 marks)*

b) Light waves carry different information to sound waves.
   Give **two** other ways in which light waves are different to sound waves.

   ....

   ....

   ....

   ....

   (2 marks)

4
marks

3 (a) The diagrams show three different rays hitting the boundary between glass and air.
The rays hit the boundary at different angles.

Complete diagram **R** to show what happens to the ray of light after it hits the boundary.

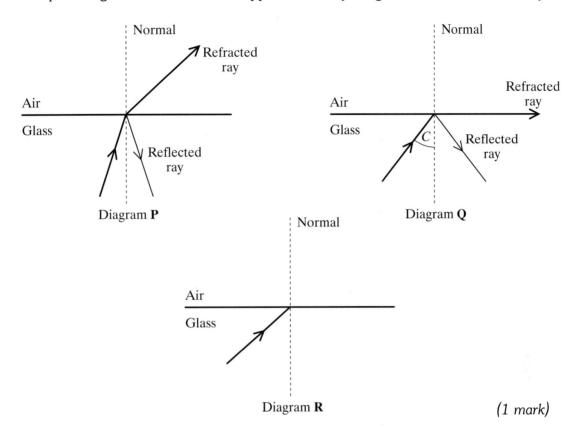

Diagram **P**

Diagram **Q**

Diagram **R**

(1 mark)

D (b) Information can be carried by light travelling along optical fibres.
The diagram shows a ray of light travelling through an optical fibre.

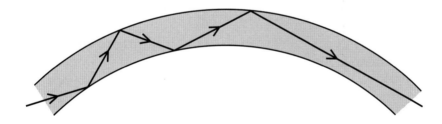

(i) Name the process by which the ray of light travels through the fibre.

....

(1 mark)

H (ii) Explain, as fully as you can, why information is sent by means of light travelling
along optical fibres, rather than by electrical signals in metal cables.

To gain full marks in this question you should write your ideas in good English.
Put them into a sensible order and use the correct scientific words.

....

....

....

....

(2 marks)

4
marks

16 The electromagnetic spectrum

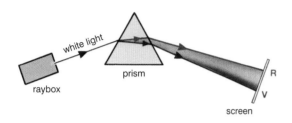

white light — raybox — prism — screen — R — V

▷ **Spectrum**

White light is *dispersed* by a prism, to form a spectrum.
The colours can be remembered by ROY G BIV.
Red is bent (deviated) the least; violet the most.

▷ **The full electromagnetic spectrum**

Visible light is just part of the full electromagnetic spectrum:

All these types of electromagnetic wave travel at the same speed through space (a vacuum).

Different wavelengths are reflected, absorbed or transmitted differently by different substances.

When the radiation is absorbed, the energy it carries:
- makes the substance hotter (e.g. when you sunbathe),
- may create an alternating current of the same frequency as the radiation (e.g. in a radio aerial),
- may cause damage to living cells.

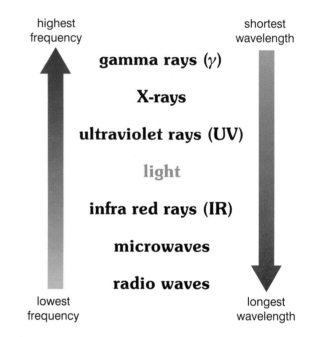

highest frequency — shortest wavelength

gamma rays (γ)

X-rays

ultraviolet rays (UV)

light

infra red rays (IR)

microwaves

radio waves

lowest frequency — longest wavelength

▷ **The effects of radiation on living cells**

- **Microwaves** are absorbed by the water in cells, which may be killed or damaged by the heat released.
- **Infra red radiation** (IR) is absorbed by the skin and is felt as heat.
- **Ultraviolet radiation** (UV) can pass through the skin to deeper tissues. The darker the skin, the more it absorbs, and less reaches deeper tissues.
- **X-rays** and **Gamma rays** (γ) mostly pass through soft tissues, but some is absorbed by the cells, which they may damage (see Topic 17).

High doses of UV, X-rays and γ-radiation can kill normal cells.
Lower doses of these radiations can cause normal cells to become cancerous.

Take care:

Be clear that the shorter the wavelength, the higher the frequency (and usually more dangerous).

Uses of electromagnetic waves

Type of radiation	Uses:	More details in *Physics for You*
Gamma rays (γ)	• to kill harmful bacteria in food • to sterilise surgical instruments • to kill cancer cells	• page 357 • page 220
X-rays	• to produce shadow pictures of materials that X-rays do not easily pass through, including bones and metals	• pages 226, 220, 318
Ultraviolet (UV)	• in sun-beds • in fluorescent tube lamps, and security coding. (Special coatings absorb the UV and emit the energy as light.)	• pages 226, 220 • page 226
Visible light	• to see this page; for plants to grow, etc	
Infra red (IR)	• in grills, toasters and radiant heaters • in optical fibre communications • for the remote control of TV sets, etc	• page 227 • page 200
Microwaves	• to send signals to and from satellites and within mobile phone networks (they pass through the atmosphere) • for cooking, because these wavelengths are strongly absorbed by water molecules in the food	• pages 320, 169 • page 227
Radio waves	• to transmit radio and TV programmes between places on the Earth's surface. (Longer waves can be reflected from the ionosphere, to go round the bend of the Earth.)	• page 221

Communications

Information signals can be sent over long distances via radio waves, cables, or optical fibres.
The signals can be sent as **analogue** signals or as **digital** signals (see the left-hand diagrams below).
Digital signals, especially in optical fibres, can carry information more quickly than analogue signals.

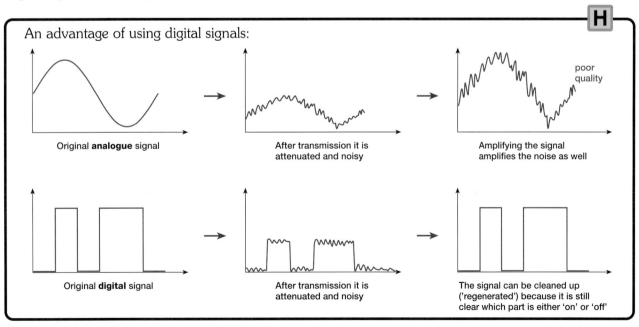

More details in *Physics for You*, pages 216–221, 226–227, 332–333, 357.

Terminal Paper Questions

1   (a) Complete the **four** spaces in the table of electromagnetic waves.

Type of wave	Use
gamma rays	....
X-rays	to produce shadow pictures of bones
....	used in sunbeds to give a suntan
light	sent along optical fibres in endoscopes
infra red rays	....
....	to communicate with satellites
radio waves	to transmit radio programmes

(4 marks)

(b) Complete the sentence by ticking (✓) the correct word.

The arrow on the left-hand side of the table above shows increasing …

frequency.   ☐

speed.   ☐

volume.   ☐

wavelength.   ☐

(1 mark)

5
marks

2 Which types of electromagnetic waves:

(a) are used to make toast?   ....

(b) are used for quick cooking?   ....

(c) are emitted by radioactive substances?   ....

(d) have the longest wavelength?   ....

(4 marks)

4
marks

3 The diagrams show four types of signal, **L**, **M**, **N** and **P**.

L

M

N

P

(a) Which of the signals, **L**, **M**, **N** and **P**, is a digital one? .... *(1 mark)*

(b) Explain, as fully as you can, why information is often sent as digital signals, rather than as analogue ones.

....

(2 marks)

———
3
marks

4 The diagram shows an astronaut. The space suit is designed to stop the Sun's dangerous electromagnetic radiation from reaching the astronaut's body.

(a) Name **two** types of electromagnetic radiation that can harm the body.

1 ....

2 ....

(2 marks)

(b) *To gain full marks in this question you should write your ideas in good English. Put them into a sensible order and use the correct scientific words.*

Explain, as fully as you can, why some types of electromagnetic radiation are harmful to the body.

....

....

....

(3 marks)

———
5
marks

17

RADIOACTIVITY

▶ **ThinkAbout:**

1. Some substances, like uranium, give out
   . . . . all the time.
   They are said to be . . . .

2. They give out 3 kinds of radiation, called
   . . . . and . . . . and . . . .
   The most penetrating of these is . . . .

▶ **Alpha, beta and gamma rays**

There are 3 types of radiation given out
(randomly) by radioactive sources:

- **alpha (α) radiation.** Easily absorbed,
  by paper or a few centimetres of air.
- **beta radiation (β)**
  Passes through air or paper, but is mostly
  absorbed by a few millimetres of metal
- **gamma (γ) radiation**
  Very penetrating, needs centimetres of lead
  or metres of concrete to absorb most of it.

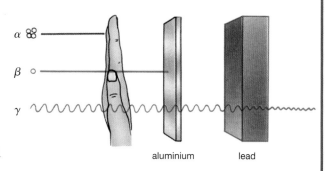

▶ **Background radiation**

There are radioactive substances all around us,
in the ground, in the air, in building materials,
in food. Radiation also reaches us from space.

▶ **Half-life**

As time goes by, the activity of a
radioactive substance decreases.

The half-life:
- is the time taken for the number of
  parent atoms in a sample to halve,
- is also the time it takes for the count
  rate to fall to half of its initial level.

You can find the half-life from a graph,
by seeing how long it takes for the activity
to fall to half.

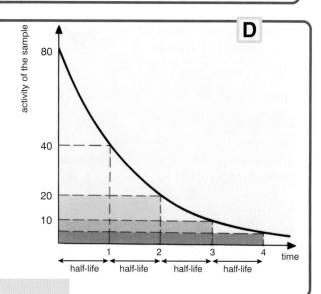

Example

The activity of some iodine-131 is 80 counts/minute.
The half-life is 8 days. What is the activity after 24 days?

After 8 days (1 half-life), the activity is 40 counts/min.
After 16 days (2 half-lives), the activity is 20 counts/min.
After 24 days (3 half-lives), the activity is 10 counts/min.

Answers: 1. radiation, radioactivity   2. alpha (α), beta (β), gamma (γ); gamma

78

▶ Effects of radiation on living tissue

When α, β or γ rays collide with neutral atoms or molecules, these may become *ionised* (charged).
In living cells this ionisation can cause damage, including cancer.
The larger the dose of radiation, the greater the risk.

When the source of radiation is *outside* the body,
- beta and gamma rays are the most dangerous because they can reach cells, to damage them.
- alpha rays are likely to be stopped by the air or by your outer skin or clothing.

Workers using radioactive sources should wear a film badge:

When the source of radiation is *inside* the body,
- alpha radiation is the most dangerous, because it is strongly absorbed, and strongly ionises.
- beta and gamma rays are less dangerous than alphas, because they are less likely to be absorbed.

Very high doses of radiation can be used to kill cancer cells and harmful microorganisms.

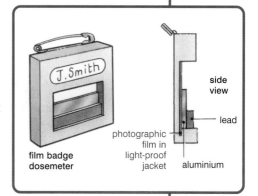

side view

lead

photographic film in light-proof jacket

aluminium

film badge dosemeter

D

▶ More uses of radiation

- **Thickness control**
  The thicker the material, the more the radiation is absorbed.
  This can be used to control the rollers to give the correct thickness:

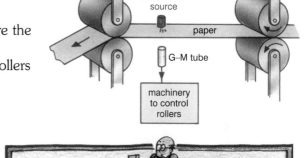

radioactive source

rollers

paper

G–M tube

machinery to control rollers

- **Tracers**
  Tracers can be used to track leaks in a pipeline:

  They can also be used for medical tests in hospital.

G-M COUNTER

LEAK

PIPELINE

▶ Using the correct radioactive source

In the pipeline shown above, it is important to use the correct radioactive isotope, so that:
- It has a half-life of only a few hours or days. This is so that it remains long enough to be detected, but not so long that it remains a safety problem.
- It is a beta-emitter. Alpha particles would be absorbed by the soil, whereas gamma-rays would pass through the metal pipe anyway.

D

H

Take care:
- Be clear about the 3 types of radiation, and their effect on the body.

- In half-life calculations, remember to subtract the background rate, if you know it.

More details in *Physics for You*, pages 350–351, 354, 356–357, 360.

Examination Questions – Radioactivity

Terminal Paper Questions

1 Radioactive substances give out radiation. There are radioactive substances all around us.

The chart shows where radiation comes from.

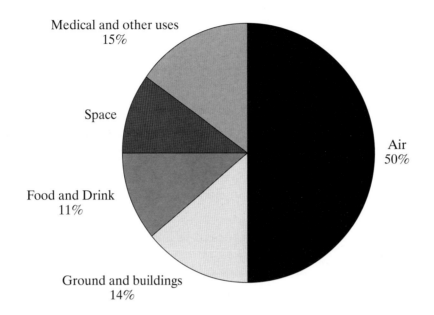

(a) (i) Complete the sentence.

Apart from medical and other uses, radiation from all of these sources is called

.... radiation. *(1 mark)*

(ii) What percentage of the radiation comes from space?
Show clearly how you worked out your answer.

....

....

Radiation from space = ... %

(2 marks)

(b) There are three types of radiation, *alpha*, *beta* and *gamma*, emitted by radioactive materials.
The diagram shows what can stop each type of radiation.

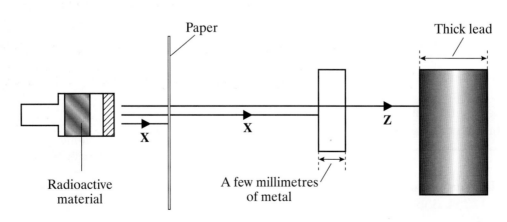

3 marks

Match the radiation, *alpha*, *beta* or *gamma*, to the statements below.

(i) **X**: The radiation is stopped by a sheet of paper. ....

(ii) **Y**: Most of the radiation is stopped by a few millimetres of metal. ....

(iii) **Z**: Most of the radiation is stopped by thick lead. ....

(2 marks)

(c) People who work with radioactive materials have to wear a special badge. One is shown below.

(i) What is inside the badge to detect radiation?

....

(1 mark)

(ii) *To gain full marks in this question you should write your ideas in good English. Put them into a sensible order and use the correct scientific words.*

Explain, as fully as you can, why large doses of radiation are dangerous.

....

....

....

....

....

....

(3 marks)

6 marks

Answers on page 116

> ### ▶ ThinkAbout:
>
> 1. Atoms have a small central . . . . , made up of protons and . . . . , around which there are . . . .
>
> 2. . . . . are positive, ... are negative, while neutrons have no . . . .
> 3. . . . . are much lighter than . . . . or . . . .

▶ Atomic structure

At one time, scientists believed in a 'plum-pudding' model of the atom. They believed that the negative electrons were stuck in a positive blob of matter.

Then Rutherford and Marsden fired alpha-particles at gold foil, which scattered them, as shown:

Rutherford showed that this means an atom has a tiny heavy positive nucleus.

We now know the nucleus is made of protons (+) and neutrons, around which are the electrons (–). In a neutral atom, the number of electrons equals the number of protons.

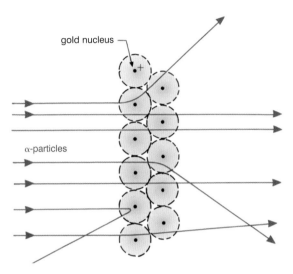

gold nucleus

α-particles

The paths of the positive alpha-particles show that they are being repelled by the positive nuclei of the atoms

	mass	charge
proton	1	+1
neutron	1	0
electron	negligible	–1

▶ Atomic number, mass number

All atoms of an element have the same number of protons. All atoms of lithium (Li) have 3, as shown:

Different elements have different numbers of protons. The number of protons in an atom is called its **atomic number** or **proton number**.

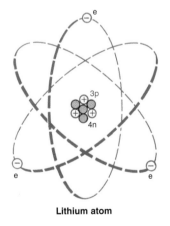

Lithium atom

Atoms of the same element can have different numbers of neutrons. These are **isotopes**. The isotope of lithium shown here has 4 neutrons. Other isotopes of lithium can have 3 or 5 neutrons.

The total number of protons + neutrons in an atom is called its **mass number** or **nucleon number**.

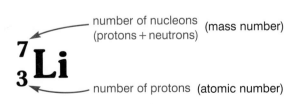

number of nucleons (mass number)
(protons + neutrons)

$$_3^7 \text{Li}$$

number of protons (atomic number)

▶ Radioactive decay

Radioactivity occurs as a result of changes in the nuclei of atoms.

A radioactive isotope ('radioisotope' or 'radionuclide') is an atom with an unstable nucleus.

When it splits up (decays):
- it emits radiation (α, β, and/or γ),
- a different atom is formed, with a different number of protons:

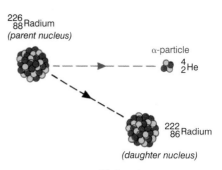

$^{226}_{88}$Radium
(parent nucleus)

α-particle
$^{4}_{2}$He

$^{222}_{86}$Radium
(daughter nucleus)

Alpha-decay
*The new atom has 2 protons (and 2 neutrons) **less than** the original atom. It is a different element.*

H

▶ Alpha, beta, gamma

- Alpha particles are helium nuclei. They are made up of 2 protons + 2 neutrons.

- Beta particles are high-speed electrons, emitted from the **nucleus** of an atom. As each electron is emitted, a neutron in the nucleus changes to become a proton.

- Gamma radiation is a wave : very short wavelength electromagnetic radiation. See Topic 16.

D **H**

▶ Nuclear fission

Nuclear fission is used to provide energy in nuclear reactors (e.g. in nuclear power stations).

When an atom with a large nucleus is bombarded with neutrons:
- the nucleus may split ('fission') into two smaller nuclei,
- further neutrons are released, which can cause a chain reaction as shown,
- the new atoms which are formed are themselves radioactive.

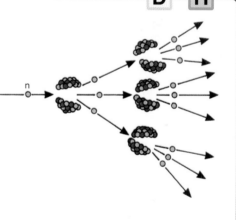

n

The energy released during radioactive decay or nuclear fission is very large compared to the energy released when a chemical bond is made between two atoms (e.g. in burning coal).

D **H**

▶ Radioactive dating

The half-life of a radioactive material is a fixed length of time. This can be used to date materials, including rocks.

For example, uranium-238 has a very long half-life, of 4500 million years. It changes slowly into a stable isotope of lead. After one half-life, half of it is unchanged and the other half has changed into lead. After 2 half-lives, $\frac{1}{4}$ of the uranium is left and $\frac{3}{4}$ is lead.

By measuring how much of the uranium in a rock has changed to lead, it is possible to calculate the age of the rock. See the examples in **Physics for You**, page 362.

Take care:
- Be clear about atomic number, mass number and isotopes.

- Be clear about the differences between alphas and betas.

More details in **Physics for You**, pages 352–353, 358–359, 362, 368.

Examination Questions
– Atomic structure, radioactive decay
Terminal Paper Questions

1 The diagram shows the 'plum pudding' model of an atom.

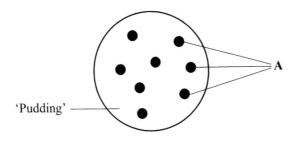

(a) Scientists thought that the 'pudding' was positively charged.

    (i) Name the particles labelled **A** in the diagram.

    .... *(1 mark)*

    (ii) Complete this sentence by choosing the correct words from the box.

negatively charged	**positively charged**	**uncharged**

    The particles labelled **A** are ....

    (1 mark)

(b) A new model of an atom was suggested by Rutherford and Marsden.
They fired alpha particles at thin metal foil.
Alpha particles are positively charged.
In their model each atom has a nucleus.

The diagram below shows the path of an alpha particle as it passes the nucleus of an atom.

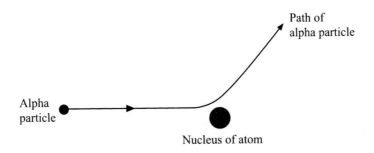

    (i) Explain why the alpha particle changes direction.

    ....

    ....

    ....

    ....

    (2 marks)

(ii) The diagram shows different paths taken by alpha particles when they were fired by Rutherford and Marsden at the thin metal foil.

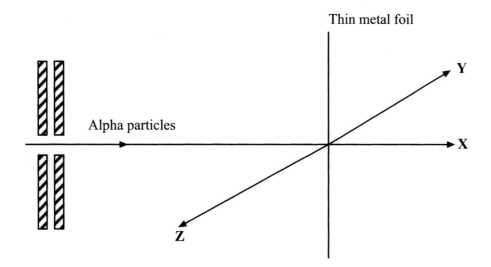

The boxes on the left show some observations from the experiment.
The boxes on the right give their explanations.
Draw a straight line from each observation to its explanation.
One has been done for you.

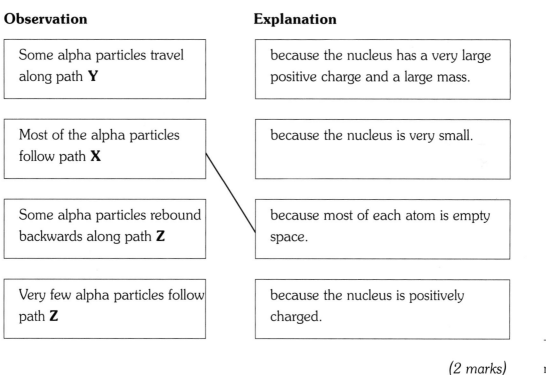

(2 marks)

6
marks

19

> ## ThinkAbout:
>
> 1. All . . . . are caused by vibrations.
> 2. The speed of sound in air is about 340 . . . . per second.
> 3. Like other waves, a sound wave transfers . . . . without transferring any matter.
> 4. Echoes are due to the . . . . of sound.
> 5. Sound can travel through solids, ... , and . . . . It cannot travel through a . . . .
> 6. A sound wave is a . . . . wave. The . . . . is transferred from molecule to . . . .

▷ Using an oscilloscope

The waveform of a sound can be displayed using a microphone and an oscilloscope:

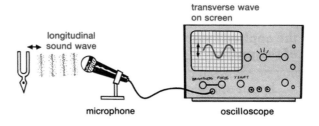

▷ Loudness and amplitude

The greater the amplitude of the vibrations, the louder the sound:

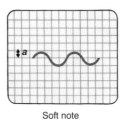

Soft note

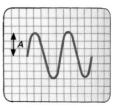

Same note but LOUDER

▷ Pitch and frequency

The number of complete vibrations in each second is called the frequency. It is measured in hertz (Hz).

The higher the frequency, the higher the pitch of the sound:

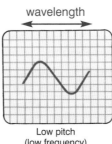

Low pitch
(low frequency)
long wavelength

High pitch
(high frequency)
short wavelength

▷ Ultrasonic waves (ultrasound)

The normal range of hearing for humans can be 20 Hz to 20 000 Hz.

Sound waves with a higher frequency than this are called ultrasonic waves. Because they have a high frequency, they have a short wavelength.

D

Like all other waves, (see Topic 15 for an example):

wave speed	**=**	**frequency**	**×**	**wavelength**
(m/s)		(hertz, Hz)		(metre, m)

Answers:

1. sounds 2. metres 3. energy 4. reflection 5. liquids, gases; vacuum 6. longitudinal; energy, molecule

86

▷ Uses of ultrasound

Ultrasonic waves can be used:
- in industry for quality control
  e.g. to detect flaws in metal castings,
- in medicine
  e.g. pre-natal scanning (ultrasound is safer than X-rays)
- in industry for cleaning dirty objects
  e.g. watches, jewellery, street lamp covers.

H

▷ Reflections

When ultrasonic waves meet a boundary between
two different media, the waves are partly reflected back.
The time taken for the reflections (echoes) to reach a detector
can be used to measure how far away the boundary is.
The results can be shown on a visual display.

H

▷ Detecting flaws in a metal casting

A transmitter is sending out pulses
of ultrasonic waves:
A receiver picks up the echoes from
different parts of the metal and
shows the results on an oscilloscope.

Pulse A is the transmitted pulse.
Pulse B has been reflected by
the flaw (b) in the metal.
Pulse C is the reflected pulse from
the end (c) of the metal block.

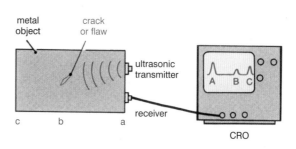

H

▷ Pre-natal scanning

When an ultrasonic wave
travels from one
substance to another
(skin, muscle, bone, fluid)
some is reflected back.
The information is used
to build up a picture of
the fetus:

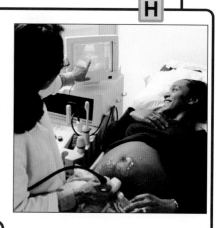

H

▷ Ultrasonic cleaning

Ultrasonic waves can be
used to shake loose the dirt
on delicate mechanisms,
without having to take them
to pieces.

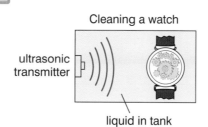

Take care:

Be careful not
to confuse
sound waves
(longitudinal) with
electromagnetic waves
(transverse), see also
Topic 16.

More details in **Physics for You**, pages 228–232, 234–235, 240–241.

Terminal Paper Questions

1   (a) **Figure 1** shows the oscilloscope trace of a note produced by a keyboard synthesiser.

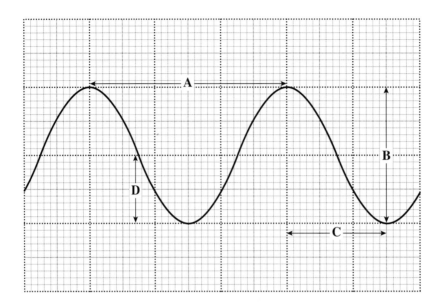

Figure 1

Which letter, **A**, **B**, **C** or **D**, labels:

(i) wavelength;   ....   *(1 mark)*

(ii) amplitude?   ....   *(1 mark)*

(b) **Figure 2** shows the oscilloscope trace of another note produced by the keyboard synthesiser.

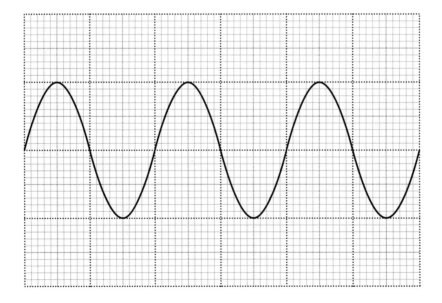

Figure 2

How would the note shown in **Figure 2** sound different from the note shown in **Figure 1**?

....

....

(1 mark)

(c) **Figure 3** shows the oscilloscope trace of another note produced by the keyboard synthesiser.

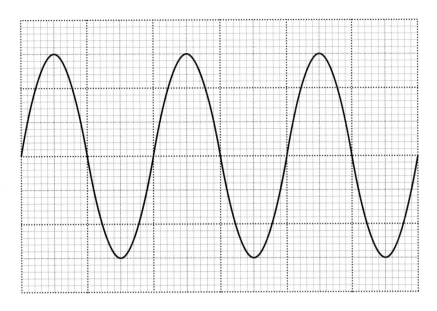

Figure 3

How would the note shown in **Figure 3** sound different from the note shown in **Figure 2**?

....

....

(1 mark)

$\dfrac{4}{\text{marks}}$

H **2** The diagram shows how ultrasonic waves can be used to clean a watch.

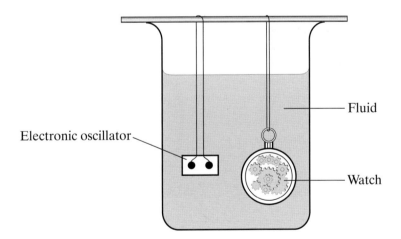

Suggest how this method cleans the watch.

....

....

....

....

(2 marks)

$\dfrac{2}{\text{marks}}$

Answers on page 116

20

The Earth

▶ **ThinkAbout:**

1. The shape of the Earth is almost . . . .
2. Inside the Earth there are . . . . main layers: the core, the . . . . , the . . . .
3. Earthquakes give out . . . . waves.
4. The crust (with the upper part of the . . . .) is divided into huge . . . . plates.

▶ **The structure of the Earth**

There are 3 main layers:

- The **core**, of about half the Earth's radius, is mostly liquid iron and nickel, but the centre is solid.
- The **mantle** has all the normal properties of a solid, but it flows slowly due to the convection currents (heated by radioactivity).
- The **crust** is a very thin layer. Its density is much less than the average density of the Earth (because the core is very dense).

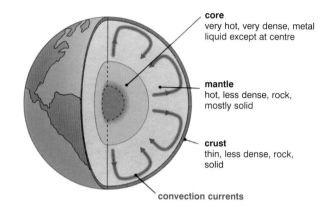

core
very hot, very dense, metal liquid except at centre

mantle
hot, less dense, rock, mostly solid

crust
thin, less dense, rock, solid

convection currents

H

▶ **Seismic waves**

We know about the inside of the Earth because of the shock waves from earthquakes, detected by using seismometers.

Earthquakes produce surface waves (that cause damage) and 2 types of wave that travel through the Earth:

- **P waves** travel fast, are longitudinal and so can travel through liquids as well as solids,
- **S waves** travel slower, are transverse and so can *only travel through solids.*

Interpreting the diagram:

1. Seismograph stations at A, B, C, D receive both P waves and S waves.
   At X and Y they receive only P waves.
   From this we know that the core is liquid, and its size can be calculated.

2. Where the P waves enter the core, there is a sudden change in direction.
   This is due to a sudden change in the speed of the P waves as they move into the liquid core. This is *refraction* (see Topic 15).

3. The paths are all curved. This is also due to refraction, as the speed of the waves changes gradually as the material gets denser.

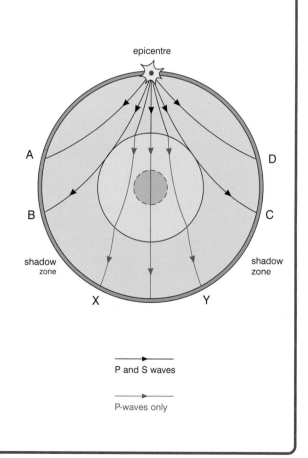

epicentre

A

D

B

C

shadow zone

shadow zone

X

Y

⟶ P and S waves

⟶ P-waves only

▶ Tectonics

Alfred Wegener (in 1915) suggested the idea of continental drift. He had some evidence for his idea:
- On maps, South America and Africa looked as if they could have fitted together as in a jig-saw.
- They have similar patterns of rock and fossils.

However his theory was not accepted for more than 50 years, until:
- Satellite (GPS) measurements showed that America and Africa are moving apart.
- Evidence was found for sea-floor spreading at mid-ocean ridges (see below).
- The idea that the Earth's lithosphere (the crust and the upper part of the mantle) is cracked into a large number of pieces, called **tectonic plates**, which move on huge convection currents.

> **Take care:**
> - Be sure that you understand why scientists came to believe Wegener's theory.
> - Be able to explain why scientists can't accurately predict earthquakes and volcanic eruptions.

▶ Earthquakes, mountains and volcanoes

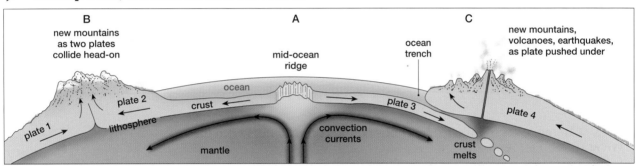

H

> ▶ **Tectonic plates** can move in 3 ways:
>
> 1. ***They may slide past each other.***
>   e.g. In California, causing earthquakes. These are very hard to predict.
>
> 2. ***They may move towards each other.***
>   e.g. At the western side of South America (the Andes).
>   See part C of the diagram above. The dense oceanic plate 3 is being subducted to move under continental plate 4. This causes earthquakes and volcanoes and changes the rock (metamorphism).
>
>   e.g. At the Himalayas.
>   See part B above, where 2 plates collide and force up new mountains.
>
> 3. ***They may move away from each other.***
>   e.g. In the mid-Atlantic ridge, with sea-floor spreading.
>   See part A above, where molten magma is rising to fill the gap as the tectonic plates move apart.
>   The sea-floor spreading was proved by the discovery of a series of magnetic stripes recording the regular reversals of the Earth's magnetic field:

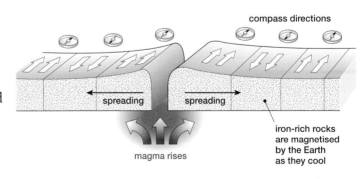

More details in **Physics for You**, pages 154–157.

Examination Questions – The Earth

Terminal Paper Questions

1 The map shows how the Earth's surface is cracked into a number of large pieces.

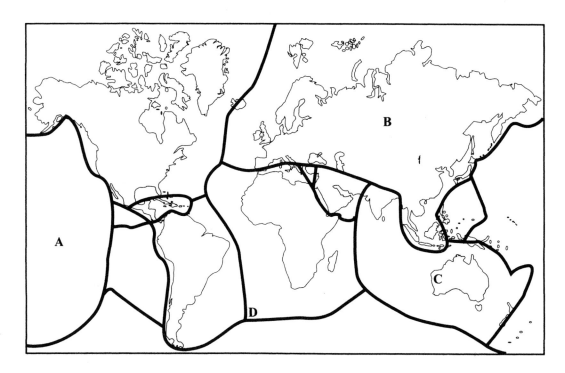

(a) Complete each sentence by choosing the correct words from the box.

crust	**lithosphere**	**mantle**	**tectonic**

The Earth's ...., which is the .... and the upper

part of the ...., is cracked into a number of large pieces. The pieces,

called .... plates, are constantly moving.

(4 marks)

(b) At which of the points, **A**, **B**, **C** or **D**, is an earthquake most likely to happen? Explain why.

....

....

(2 marks)

(c) Scientists study earthquakes and the shock waves which they produce.
They use the data they obtain to help them to predict earthquakes.

Put a cross (✗) next to the statement that is **incorrect**.

Earthquakes and volcanoes occur in similar places. ☐

It is easy to predict in which region earthquakes will occur. ☐

It is easy to predict when earthquakes will occur. ☐

Scientists use seismometers to study earthquake waves. ☐   *(1 mark)*

7 marks

H 2 The drawing shows how seismic waves (shock waves from earthquakes) are recorded.

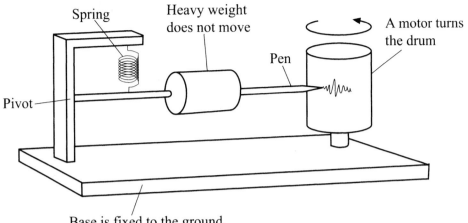

(a) Two types of wave, **P** and **S**, travel from the earthquake through the Earth.
State the differences between **P** and **S** waves.

....

....

(3 marks)

(b) The diagrams show **P** and **S** waves meeting the boundary between two layers of the Earth.

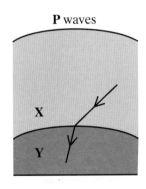

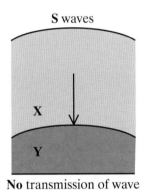

(i) What happens to the **P** waves at the boundary?

....

(1 mark)

(ii) Explain what the behaviour of the **P** and **S** waves at the boundary tells you about layer **X** and layer **Y**.

....

....

....

....

(3 marks)

7 marks

Answers on page 116

Getting the Grades – Waves and Radiation

Try this question, then compare your answer with the two examples opposite ▶

1   (a) The diagram shows, in a simplified form, how a telephone call can be transmitted from Britain to the USA.

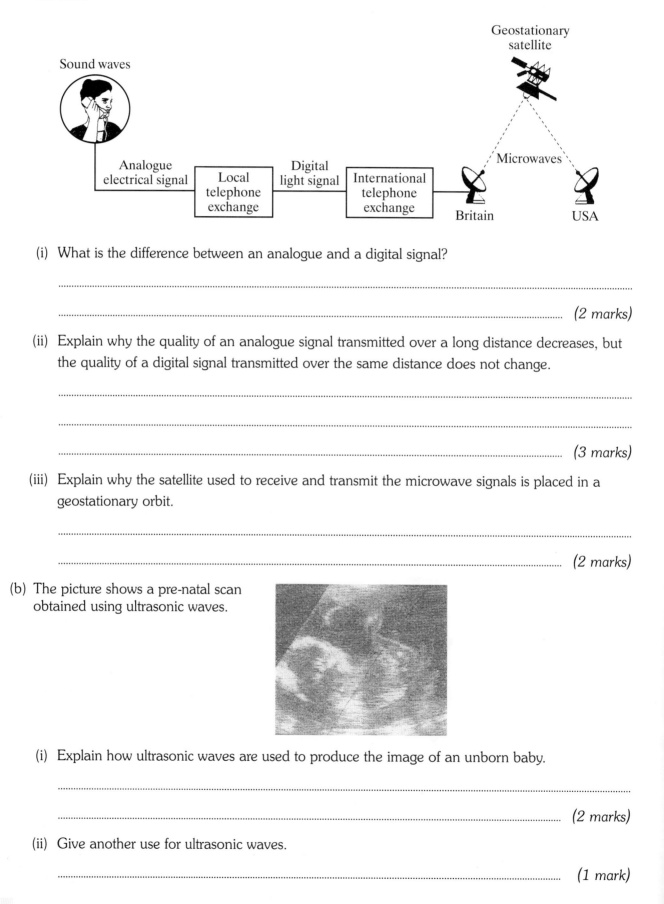

(i) What is the difference between an analogue and a digital signal?

....

.... *(2 marks)*

(ii) Explain why the quality of an analogue signal transmitted over a long distance decreases, but the quality of a digital signal transmitted over the same distance does not change.

....

....

.... *(3 marks)*

(iii) Explain why the satellite used to receive and transmit the microwave signals is placed in a geostationary orbit.

....

.... *(2 marks)*

(b) The picture shows a pre-natal scan obtained using ultrasonic waves.

(i) Explain how ultrasonic waves are used to produce the image of an unborn baby.

....

.... *(2 marks)*

(ii) Give another use for ultrasonic waves.

.... *(1 mark)*

GRADE 'A' ANSWER

Daniel has correctly described both signals so gains both marks.

Daniel has made two correct points so gets two of the marks. He should have explained that the signals will need amplifying to travel over a long distance. He could also have said that noise in digital signals is low amplitude and treated as 'off'.

Daniel

1 (a) (i) A digital signal is on or off. ✔ An analogue signal has an amplitude that varies continuously. ✔

(ii) Noise gets amplified in analogue signals ✔ In digital signals the shape of the pulses is changed but not the on off pattern. ✔

(iii) In a geostationary orbit the satellite is always in the same point in the sky ✔ so the receiving dishes can always point to the same point in the sky and get a signal. ✔

(b) (i) Ultrasound waves are reflected back to a receiver each time they move between different tissues in the body. ✔

(ii) Ultrasonic waves can be used to break up kidney stones without needing surgery. ✔

To get the second mark Daniel should explain that the time taken for the reflected wave to reach the receiver is used to produce the image.

This is a correct use for ultrasound.

8 marks = Grade A answer

▶ **Improve your Grades   A up to A***

To get an A* grade it is important to give very full information in response to each question, especially in those questions that ask you to 'explain'.

GRADE 'C' ANSWER

Amy has correctly described a digital signal but she has not explained how it is different from an analogue signal, so she gets just 1 mark.

Amy

1 (a) (i) A digital signal is just on or off. ✔

(ii) When analogue signals are amplified ✔ noise gets amplified ✔ but it doesn't in digital signals.

(iii) A geostationary orbit means the satellite is always over the same point on the Earth. ✔

(b) (i) Ultrasound waves bounce back off the baby and they are used to make a picture of it. ✗

(ii) They can be used to clean delicate things like watches. ✔

Amy has made two correct points so she gets two of the three marks.

Amy has not really given any new information, she has just repeated the question so this does not get any marks.

This is a correct use for ultrasound so she gets the mark.

To gain the second mark Amy needs to say that this means that transmitting and receiving dishes do not need to keep changing direction.

5 marks = Grade C answer

▶ **Improve your Grades   C up to B**

Remember that you must give new information in your answers, not just put the question into different words.
If you are asked to give the difference between two things you must describe them both to show what the difference is.

Electronic control circuits

▶ **ThinkAbout** what these components do:

1. LED: 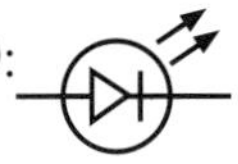   2. LDR: 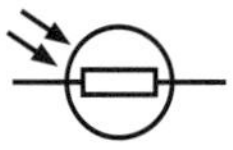   3. Relay: (normally open type) 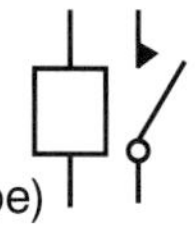   4. Capacitor:

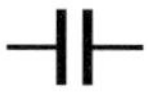

▶ **An electronic system has 3 parts:**

| input sensor |—| processor |—| output device |

e.g. thermistor, LDR, switches for pressure or tilt, etc.

e.g. logic gates (AND, OR, NOT)

e.g. lamps, LEDs, bells, motors, heaters (may be switched by a transistor and relay)

▶ A **relay** is a switch. A small (input) current in the coil switches on a large (output) current.

▶ **Resistor code**

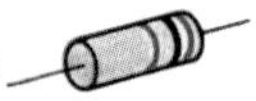

Make sure you can use the colour code for resistors.

▶ **Logic gates**   There are 3 kinds, each with a 'truth table':

AND gate

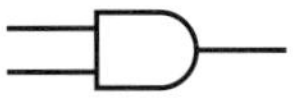

1st input	2nd input	Output
0	0	0
1	0	0
0	1	0
1	1	1

OR gate

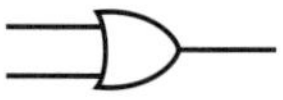

1st input	2nd input	Output
0	0	0
1	0	1
0	1	1
1	1	1

NOT gate

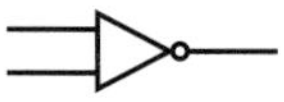

Input	Output
0	1
1	0

Logic gates can be combined, as shown in the example:

You may be asked to work out a truth table showing the output of a combination of up to 3 gates with up to 3 inputs.

Example

Draw a truth table for this combination:

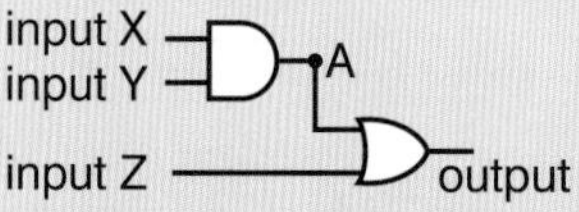

input X
input Y
   A
input Z ————— output

Work through the answers shown, and check that you understand each part.

input X	input Y	so, at A (AND)	input Z	Output (OR)
0	0	0	0	0
1	0	0	0	0
0	1	0	0	0
1	1	1	0	1
0	0	0	1	1
1	0	0	1	1
0	1	0	1	1
1	1	1	1	1

▶ **Capacitors**

The diagram shows a capacitor in a circuit:

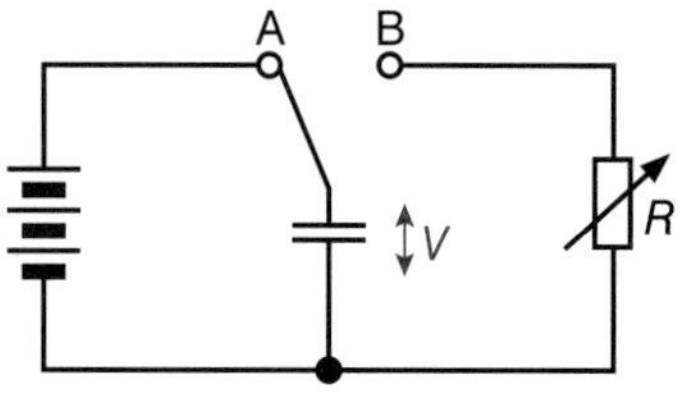

When the switch is first moved to position A, a current flows, and the voltage V increases, and charge is stored in the capacitor.
When the switch is moved to position B, the capacitor discharges, current flows through the resistor R, and the voltage V decreases.
The *time* for the capacitor to charge or discharge increases if:
- the resistance R is increased,
- the value of the capacitor is increased.
This can be used in a timing circuit (see opposite page).

▷ Potential divider circuits

In the circuit shown, the output p.d. (V_{out}) is a fraction of the input p.d. (V_{in}).
V_{out} can be calculated by:

$$V_{out} = V_{in} \times \frac{R_2}{R_1 + R_2}$$

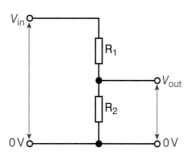

Example

In the circuit shown, V_{in} = 6 V, R_1 = 100 Ω and R_2 = 200 Ω. What is the size of V_{out}?

$$V_{out} = V_{in} \cdot \times \frac{R_2}{R_1 + R_2}$$

$$= 6 \text{ V} \times \frac{200}{100 + 200} = 4 \text{ V}$$

H

▷ A light-dependent switch

This circuit will switch on a lamp (e.g. a street lamp) when it goes dark. This is how it works:

- The LDR and the resistor form a potential divider circuit.
- Initially, in daytime, the resistance of the LDR is low, so V_{out} is high. Because the NOT gate inverts it, the voltage level at the transistor switch is low, so the transistor is off ... and so the lamp is off.
- As dusk arrives, the resistance of the LDR increases, so V_{out} becomes low. The NOT gate inverts this, so the transistor is switched on and a current passes through the relay ... which switches on the lamp.

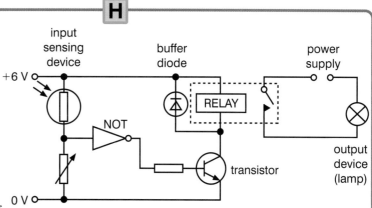

The transistor acts as an electronic switch.

To protect the transistor when the relay is switched off, a diode is placed across the relay as shown.

This circuit can be modified to do a different job, e.g. to switch on a heater as the temperature falls, just change the LDR to be a thermistor.

H

▷ A time delay switch

In this circuit:

- Initially the capacitor C is uncharged and V = 0, so the transistor is off.
- When the switch S is closed, a current flows through R, and the capacitor slowly charges up. V increases and eventually switches on the transistor and the lamp, after a *time delay* (which depends on the values of R and C).

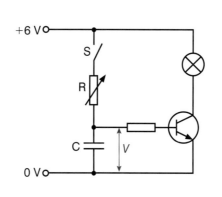

Take care:

- Work logically through a truth table.

- When analysing circuits, first identify the potential divider.

- Then see the effect of any logic gates.

Make sure you can discuss the advantages and disadvantages of: • CCTV • mobile phones • the internet

H

More details in **Physics for You**, pages 324–331, 336–339, 264.

Examination Questions – Electronic control circuits

Module Test Questions

1 Match words from the list with each of the symbols **1–4**.

AND gate

capacitor

LED

relay

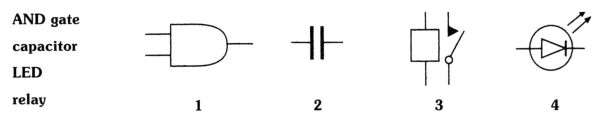

2 This electronic system shows how a fan can be turned on when it is hot in summer during the day.

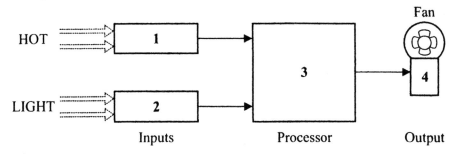

Match the device in the list that is most suitable for each part **1–4**.

AND gate

light sensor

motor

temperature sensor

⊞ **3** In any sensor circuit, when the voltage (V_{out}) becomes large enough (high), the input to the processor is high.

Match each sensor circuit, **1–4**, with its description.

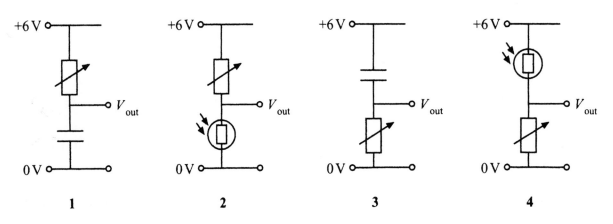

L	When the surroundings become dark, V_{out} goes high
M	When the surroundings become bright V_{out} goes high
N	V_{out} starts high, but may go low after a time delay
P	V_{out} starts low, but may go high after a time delay

12
marks

Terminal Paper Questions

1 (a) The circuit contains a lamp and two switches, S_1 and S_2.

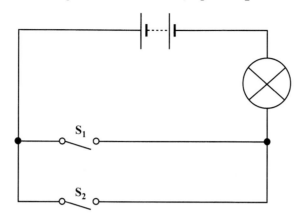

(i) Complete the truth table for the above circuit.

Switch S_1	Switch S_2	Lamp
OFF (0)	OFF (0)	OFF (0)
ON (1)	OFF (0)	
OFF (0)	ON (1)	
ON (1)	ON (1)	

(1 mark)

(ii) Which type of logic gate produces this truth table?

....

(1 mark)

(b) The diagram shows an electronic system used to switch on a heater in a greenhouse.

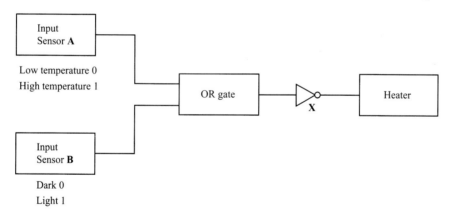

What is:

(i) **X**;   ....

(ii) input sensor **A**;   ....

(iii) input sensor **B**?   ....   *(3 marks)*

(c) When will the heater be ON?
Explain your answer.

....

....

(3 marks)

8
marks

Moments, Momentum, Circular Motion

▷ **ThinkAbout:**

1. The turning effect (or . . . .) on a spanner depends upon the . . . . applied and on the . . . . from the nut to the force.

2. The centre of mass (centre of . . . .) of a metre rule is at the . . . . of the rule.

3. An object balances at its centre of . . . .

▷ **Finding the centre of mass of a card**

A suspended object comes to rest with its centre of mass below the pivot. Then the weight does not exert a turning effect (moment).

Hanging the card twice, with a plumbline, allows you to find the centre of mass:

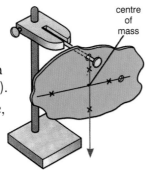

centre of mass

H

▷ **Stable and unstable objects**

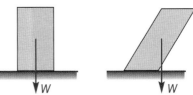

If the line of action of the weight (W) lies outside the base of the object, there is a moment, and the object tends to fall over.

▷ **Calculating moments**

The size of a moment (turning effect) can be calculated by:

moment	=	force	×	perpendicular distance (from line of action to pivot)
(Nm)		(newton, N)		(metre, m)

H

▷ **The law of moments**

If an object is not turning, the moments must be balanced, so:

In equilibrium:

| total anti-clockwise moment | = | total clockwise moment |

Example 1

A metre rule is balanced at its centre. How big is the force X?

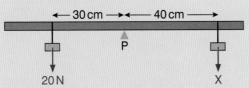

← 30 cm → ← 40 cm →

20 N   X

$$\frac{\text{total moment}}{\text{anti-clockwise}} = \frac{\text{total moment}}{\text{clockwise}}$$

20 N × 30 cm = X × 40 cm

∴ X = <u>15 N</u>

Example 2

A metre rule is balanced, but not at its centre. What is the weight (W) of the rule?

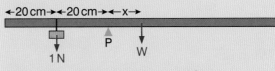

← 20 cm → ← 20 cm → ← x →

1 N   W

Since W is at the centre, x = 10 cm.

$$\frac{\text{total moment}}{\text{anti-clockwise}} = \frac{\text{total moment}}{\text{clockwise}}$$

1 N × 20 cm = W × 10 cm

∴ W = <u>2 N</u>

Answers: 3. mass   2. gravity, centre

1. moment, force, distance

Take care: Make sure you can explain all the steps of the 'card' experiment.

Momentum

The momentum of an object depends only on its mass and velocity. It is a vector quantity: it has both size (magnitude) and direction.

momentum	=	mass	×	velocity
(kg m/s)		(kg)		(m/s)

H

 ### Changing momentum

When a force acts on a movable object, it changes the object's momentum:

$$\text{force (N)} = \frac{\text{change in momentum (kg m/s)}}{\text{time that force acts (s)}}$$

Example

A golf ball has a mass of 0.05 kg. A golfer hits a still ball with a force of 500 N for 0.01 s. What is then the velocity of the golf ball?

$$\text{force} = \frac{\text{change in momentum}}{\text{time}}$$

$$500 \text{ N} = \frac{0.05 \text{ kg} \times \text{velocity}}{0.01 \text{ s}} \qquad \text{so velocity} = \frac{500 \text{ N} \times 0.01 \text{ s}}{0.05 \text{ kg}} = \underline{100 \text{ m/s}}$$

H

Collisions (and explosions)

When 2 objects collide (e.g. snooker balls), they each exert a force on the other.

The total momentum stays the same.

Usually the kinetic energy is *less* after a collision. It is not 'conserved'. Some energy is transferred to heat, sound, etc.

However in an elastic collision (e.g. between gas molecules) kinetic energy is conserved.

total momentum before a collision	=	total momentum after the collision

Example

In an accident, car A (mass 1500 kg) travelling at 10 m/s bumps into the back of stationary car B (mass 1000 kg). Car A is slowed to 4 m/s. At what velocity v does car B jerk forward?

total momentum before = total momentum after

$$(1500 \text{ kg} \times 10 \text{ m/s}) + 0 = (1500 \text{ kg} \times 4 \text{ m/s}) + (1000 \text{ kg} \times v)$$

$$15\,000 \text{ kg m/s} = 6000 \text{ kg m/s} + (1000 \text{ kg} \times v)$$

$$\text{so velocity } v = \frac{9000 \text{ kg m/s}}{1000 \text{ kg}} = \underline{9 \text{ m/s}}$$

 ## Circular motion

An object moving in a circle at constant *speed* is changing its direction all the time, so its *velocity* is changing. It is accelerating, so a **centripetal** force is needed:

The centripetal force will need to be greater if:
- the mass of the object is greater,
- the speed of the object is greater,
- the radius of the circle is smaller.

In the Solar System, the centripetal force for an orbit is provided by the gravitational attraction between masses.

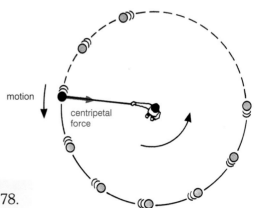

More details in **Physics for You**, pages 100–106, 144–146, 78.

Examination Questions
– Moments, Momentum, Circular Motion

Terminal Paper Questions

1   (a)   The diagram shows three vehicles, **A**, **B** and **C**, travelling along a road at 20 m/s.

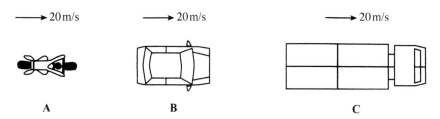

A   B   C

Which vehicle, **A**, **B** or **C**, has the greatest momentum?
Give the reason for your answer.

Vehicle: ....

Reason: ....

....

(2 marks)

(b)   The next diagram shows three racing cars, **D**, **E** and **F**, all with the same mass,
travelling at different speeds along the straight part of the track.

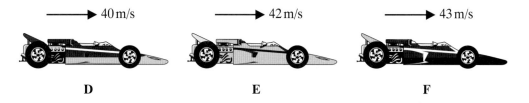

D   E   F

Which racing car, **D**, **E** or **F**, has the greatest momentum?
Give the reason for your answer.

Vehicle: ....

Reason: ....

....

(2 marks)

(c)   Racing car **D** has a mass of 1250 kg.
Calculate its momentum.
Write down the equation you are going to use.

....

(1 mark)

Show clearly how you work out your answer, and include the unit.

....

....

....

Momentum = ...

(3 marks)

8
marks

2 The diagram shows an overhead view of a door.

The door is fixed to the door frame by a hinge. It can be opened by applying a force of 30 N.

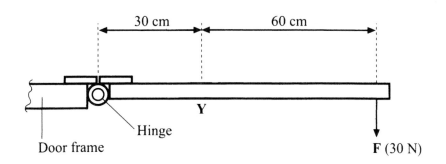

(a) (i) Complete the **three** spaces to give the equation which is used to calculate the turning effect of a force.

.... = ... × perpendicular ....

between line of action and pivot.

(1 mark)

(ii) Calculate the turning effect of the force, **F**, in the diagram.

Show clearly how you work out your answer.

....

....

....

....

Moment = ... Ncm

(2 marks)

(b) Someone pushes the door open by applying a force at **Y**. The force needed to open the door is **not** 30 N. Explain why the force needed to open the door is different.

....

....

....

....

(2 marks)

5 marks

Answers on page 117

LENSES

▷ **ThinkAbout:**

1. When light travels into a glass block, the rays are bent . . . . the normal line. This is called . . . .

2. When light travels out of glass into air, the . . . . are refracted . . . . from the . . . . This happens because of a change in . . . .

▷ **Lenses**

There are 2 kinds of lenses:

- **Converging** (convex) lens
  This converges rays of light (so that the rays come closer together):

  Parallel rays of light are converged to meet at a point F, the principal focus. The distance from the lens to F is called the focal length.

- **Diverging** (concave) lens
  In a diverging lens, the rays are refracted so that they diverge away from each other:

  They diverge away from the principal focus, F.

parallel rays of light

F

f
(focal length)

Convex (converging) lens

parallel rays of light

F

f
(focal length)

Concave (diverging) lens

▷ **Images**

Images can be:
- **Real**. The light rays go through the image (like the converging lens above, and the camera below).
- **Virtual**. The light rays do not actually go through the image (like in a plane mirror, or the focus of the diverging lens shown here).

Images can also be:
- erect or inverted (upside-down),
- magnified or diminished.

▷ **Camera**

In a camera, a converging lens is used to produce a real image of an object, on the film:

Compared to the object, the image is nearer to the lens and so it is smaller.

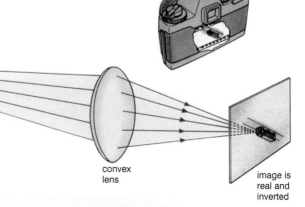

convex lens

image is real and inverted

Answers: 1. towards, refraction   2. rays/waves, away, normal; speed (velocity)

▷ Ray diagrams for lenses

There are 2 constructions to use, to find the image:

① Parallel rays of light are refracted to go through the principal focus F.

② Rays of light going through the centre of the lens travel straight on.

The points marked '2F' are twice as far from the lens as the points marked F (the focus).

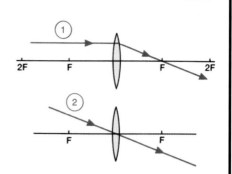

▷ In a camera

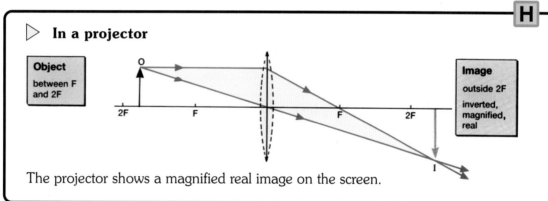

Distant Object
outside 2F

Image
between F and 2F
inverted, diminished, real

This is the same example as in the camera diagram on the opposite page.
A real image, diminished in size, is shown on the film.

▷ In a projector

Object
between F and 2F

Image
outside 2F
inverted, magnified, real

The projector shows a magnified real image on the screen.

▷ In a magnifying glass

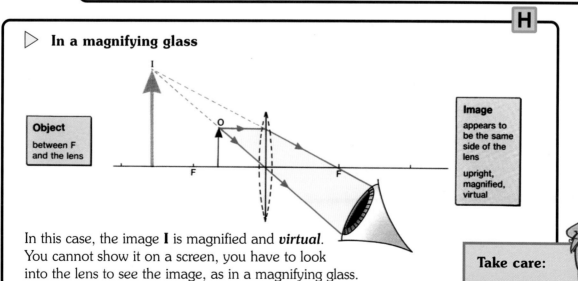

Object
between F and the lens

Image
appears to be the same side of the lens
upright, magnified, virtual

In this case, the image **I** is magnified and **virtual**.
You cannot show it on a screen, you have to look into the lens to see the image, as in a magnifying glass.

Take care:

Draw rays accurately, so the straight lines go exactly through the key points.

More details in **Physics for You**, pages 202–207.

Module Test Questions

1 Which **two** of the lenses shown could be used in a simple camera?

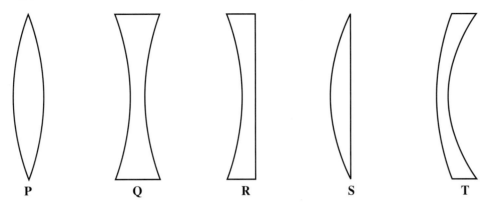

2 A ray box gives three parallel rays of light which pass through lens **X**. The paths of the rays are traced. The experiment is repeated for lens **Y**.

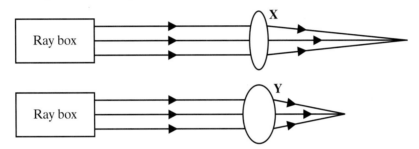

Choose the correct word from the list for each of the spaces **1–4** in the passage.

less	more	longer	shorter

Lens **X** converges light ....**1**...... because parallel rays meet at a ......**2**...... distance from the lens.

Lens **Y** converges light ....**3**...... because parallel rays meet at a ....**4**....... distance from the lens.

3 A student uses a converging lens to form an image of distant clouds on a blank sheet of paper.

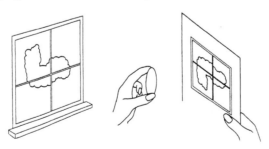

Match the missing words from the list with the spaces **1–4** below.

focal	real	parallel	sharp

The rays of light from the distant clouds are almost ......**1**...... .

Because the light rays meet, the image formed on the paper is called a ....**2**...... image.

The student moves the paper to where the image is most ......**3**....... .

This place is close to the ......**4**...... point of the lens.

10
marks

Terminal Paper Questions

1 The diagram shows side views of six pieces of glass.

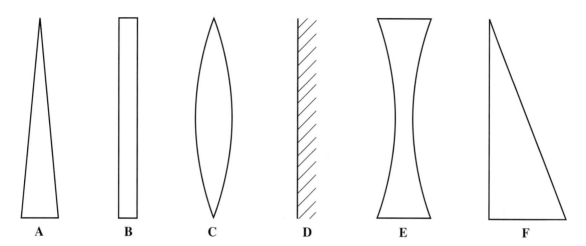

(a) Which of **A**, **B**, **C**, **D**, **E** or **F** is:

(i) a converging lens; ....

(ii) a diverging lens? ....

(2 marks)

(b) Complete the path of the **two** rays of light to show what happens when they pass through **C**.

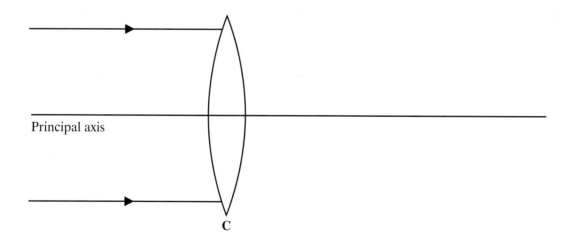

(3 marks)

5 marks

Examination answers and tips

TOPIC 1 – Conduction, Convection, Radiation

Module Test Questions

1 A and E

2 1 – kinetic energy

2 – free electrons

3 – density

4 – waves

3 1 – electrons

2 – collisions

3 – ions

4 – waves

Terminal Paper Questions

1 (a) (i) through the walls   1

(ii) carpets   1

(iii) double glazing   1

(b) draught proofing   1

it has the shortest payback time   1

payback time is 6 months   1

Examiner's Tip ✓
Work out each payback time to find which is the shortest, this will be the most cost-effective thing to fit.
Payback time = cost/money saved per year.

TOPIC 2 – Using electricity

Module Test Questions

1 1 – movement (kinetic energy)

2 – heat (thermal energy)

3 – light

4 – sound

2 2.1 A

2.2 C

Terminal Paper Questions

1 (a) No. Units   = power in kW × time in hours

     = 1.5 × 0.5 = 0.75   1

(b) 1 kW   = 1000 W

1.5 kW   = 1.5 × 1000

1.5 kW   = 1500 W   1

(c) 30 minutes

     = 30 × 60 seconds

     = 1800 seconds   1

(d) No. joules = power in watts × time in seconds

     = 1500 × 1800

     = 2 700 000   1

Examiner's Tip ✓
A kilowatt-hour is also called a 'Unit'. It is a measure of electrical energy.
To calculate energy in Units, power must be in kilowatts and time in hours.
To calculate energy in joules, power must be in watts and time in seconds.

2 (a) No. units used = later reading − earlier reading

     = 39984 − 38017

     = 1967   1

(b) Cost   = number of Units × cost per Unit

     = 1967 × 8p = 15736p

     = £157.36   1

Examiner's Tip ✓
Remember to divide the cost in pence by 100 to get an answer in pounds.

3 (a) charge = current × time   1

     = 0.25 A × 60 × 60 s   1

     = 900 C   1

(b) energy transferred = p.d. × charge

     = 230 V × 900 C   1

     = 207 000 J   1

Examiner's Tip ✓
In calculations always set your answers out as shown above. Even if the final answer is wrong you will gain credit from correct working.

Examination answers and tips

TOPIC 3 – Energy transfers

Module Test Questions

1 1 – 100 J

     2 – 5 J

     3 – 95 J

     4 – 5%

Examiner's Tip ✓

Remember that the power (in watts) is the energy transferred (in joules) each second.

2 2.1 B

     2.2 D

Terminal Paper Questions

1	(a)	(i) light	1
		(ii) electrical …movement (kinetic)	2
		(iii) gravitational potential	1
	(b) heat		1

Examiner's Tip ✓

Energy never disappears, it is transferred to other forms. Wasted energy is usually transferred as heat.

TOPIC 4 – Energy resources

Module Test Questions

1 1 – solar cells

     2 – nuclear power station

     3 – tidal barrage

     4 – hydroelectric dam

2 1 – uranium

     2 – coal

     3 – geothermal

     4 – hydrolectric

3 geothermal energy sources

     nuclear power stations

Terminal Paper Questions

1 Advantage of using wind:

The energy source is free.   1

Disadvantage of using wind:

48 000 wind turbines may be needed to supply the UK demand.   1

Advantage of using coal:

The UK demand could be supplied by only 48 coal-fired power stations.   1

Disadvantage of using coal:

The power station produces sulphur dioxide gas which gives rise to acid rain.   1

Examiner's Tip ✓

Do not forget to make use of the information given in the question.

Make sure that you give separate reasons. For example, saying energy from wind is free and then saying energy from coal is not free, does not count as two separate reasons.

Examination answers and tips

TOPIC 5 – Circuits

Module Test Questions

1 1 – resistor

2 – diode

3 – switch

4 – fuse

2 1 – diode

2 – LDR

3 – cell

4 – switch

3 B and D are **false**

Terminal Paper Questions

1 (a) $V = I \times R$

$$R = \frac{V}{I}$$ 1

$$R = \frac{230\ V}{3\ A}$$

$$R = 77\ \Omega$$ 1

(b) $V = I \times R$

$$I = \frac{V}{R}$$ 1

$$I = \frac{230\ V}{45\ A}$$

$$I = 5.1\ A$$ 1

Examiner's Tip ✓

Practise transposing formulae for the higher tier questions.

Or you may find it easier to put the numbers in the equation first of all.

These answers have been rounded to 2 significant figures. Always try to give your answer to the same number of significant figures as the data provided in the question.

TOPIC 6 – Magnetic effect of a current

Module Test Questions

1 1.1 D

1.2 C

1.3 C

Terminal Paper Questions

1 (a) 1. Reverse the poles of the magnets. 1

2. Reverse the direction of the current. 1

Examiner's Tip ✓

To get the mark you must say 'reverse' the current, not just 'change' the current.

(b) 1. Increase the current. 1

2. Increase the strength of the magnetic field. 1

Examiner's Tip ✓

Increasing the strength of the magnetic field means using a stronger magnet or reducing the gap between the magnets. You could also increase the size of the forces by increasing the number of turns on the coil.

2 B – Iron arm 1

C – Pivot 1

D – Spring 1

E – Coil 1

Examiner's Tip ✓

The diagram of the circuit breaker may not be exactly the same as one that you have seen before, but it will work in the same way. Learn the parts carefully and you will be able to work out which is which on any diagram.

Examination answers and tips

TOPIC 7 – Static electricity

Module Test Questions

1 1 – electrons

2 – negatively charged

3 – positively charged

4 – discharged

Examiner's Tip ✓
Remember: only electrons can be removed by friction.

2 R and T are correct

Terminal Paper Questions

1 (a) smoke particles become charged (+)   1

by losing electrons   1

smoke particles repelled by grid (+)   1

and are attracted to negative plates   1

particles stick to plate   1

Examiner's Tip ✓
Remember that it is only electrons that are transferred from one body to another. If a body loses electrons it becomes positively charged. If it gains electrons it becomes negatively charged.

(b) photocopier   1

(c) pipes may become charged   1

spark may jump to earth   1

could ignite petrol vapour   1

Examiner's Tip ✓
Three marks means you must give three distinct points.

TOPIC 8 – Mains electricity

Module Test Questions

1 A and C are true

2 1 – DVD player is not earthed

2 – wrong fuse is used

3 – cable is loose

4 – live wire is incorrectly connected

3 3.1 C

3.2 D

Examiner's Tip ✓
Learn the diagram of the 3-pin plug carefully. It can appear in questions in lots of different ways.

Terminal Paper Questions

1 (a) if live wire touches the metal case   1

current flows to earth through the live wire   1

instead of through a person   1

(b) fuse should be in the live wire   1

so when fuse blows, appliance is no longer live   1

(c) (i) fuse value needs to be higher

or it would melt/blow in normal use   1

(ii) slightly higher or it would take too long to melt/blow   1

(d) can be easily re-set   1

Examiner's Tip ✓
Remember that fuses take some time to melt. Circuit breakers can be used to switch off appliances much more quickly.

Examination answers and tips

TOPIC 9 – Electromagnetic induction

Module Test Questions

1 1.1 D
    1.2 B
    1.3 C
    1.4 A

Examiner's Tip ✓

Remember that transformers only work on a.c. The voltage is transformed up to a high voltage for transmission across the National Grid, but transformed down to a lower voltage for domestic use.

Terminal Paper Questions

1 (a)

Diagram 2   1

Diagram 3   1

Examiner's Tip ✓

If the direction of the movement of the magnet is reversed, the current is reversed.

(b) 1. Increase the speed of rotation of the magnet. 1

   2. Increase the number of turns of the coil   1

TOPIC 10 – Velocity and acceleration

Terminal Paper Questions

1 (a) Plot 4 points correctly (lose 1 for each incorrect plot)   2

   Draw a line of best fit through the points   1

Examiner's Tip ✓

Plot points on graphs carefully with a sharp pencil. Check which way round the axes are.

When drawing a line (or curve) of best fit, try to balance the points above and below the line (ignore any obviously-wrong points).

If the graph is a straight-line, do not just join the first and last points (because they are no more reliable than any other points).

(b) (i) 50 m   1

   (ii) 1.5 s   1

(c) ~~slowing down~~

   moving at a steady speed

   ~~speeding up~~   1

2 (a) acceleration = gradient   1

$$= \frac{40}{8}$$ 1

$$= 5 \text{ m/s}^2$$ 2

Examiner's Tip ✓

You must include the unit with your answer to get all of the marks.

(b) distance = area under the graph from 18 to 22 seconds   1

$$= \tfrac{1}{2} \times \text{base} \times \text{height (of triangle)}$$

$$= \tfrac{1}{2} \times 4 \times 40$$ 1

$$= 80 \text{ m}$$ 1

Examination answers and tips

TOPIC 11 – Forces

Terminal Paper Questions

1 B and D   1

   B and D   1

   C   1

2 (a) Both the thinking and the braking distances
        increase with increasing speed.   2

   (b) (i) 1. Drinking alcohol (or taking drugs)   1

             2. Tiredness   1

      (ii) 1. Worn tyres   1

             2. Worn brakes   1

Examiner's Tip ✓

*No marks will be awarded for just saying 'tyres'
or 'brakes'. Remember to say what it is about the
condition of the tyres or brakes that would
increase the braking distance. Increasing the
speed would also increase the braking distance.*

3 (a) $F = m \times a$

$$a = \frac{F}{m}$$ 1

$$= \frac{5\,\text{N}}{20\,\text{kg}}$$ 1

$$= 0.25\ \text{m/s}^2$$ 1

   (b) acceleration = change in speed/time taken
                for the change

   speed after 8 seconds

              = acceleration $\times$ time   1

              = 0.25×8 1

              = 2 m/s   1

Examiner's Tip ✓

Always remember to show your working.

*Even if the final answer is wrong, you will gain
some credit from correct working.*

TOPIC 12 – Work and energy

Terminal Paper Questions

1 (a) work done = force $\times$ distance moved   1

               = 200 N $\times$ 3 m   1

               = 600 J   1

   (b) (i) weight = mass $\times$ gravitational field strength   1

               = 60 kg $\times$ 10 N/kg

               = 600 N   1

      (ii) There is friction between the crate and
          the slope   1
          so more work is done sliding the crate
          because lifting does no work against
          friction   1

2 (a) (i) kinetic energy = $\frac{1}{2} \times$ mass $\times$ speed^2 1

      (ii) speed^2 = $2 \times \dfrac{\text{ke}}{\text{mass}}$

$$= 2 \times \frac{225\,000\,\text{J}}{2000\,\text{kg}}$$ 1

$$= 225$$

        speed = 15 m/s   1

Examiner's Tip ✓

*Practice rearranging equations. Do not forget to
find the square root at the end to find the speed.*

   (b) (i) change in gpe = weight $\times$ h   1
      (ii) h = change in gpe/weight
           = $225\,000/2000 \times 10$ 1
           = 11.25 m   1

Examiner's Tip ✓

*Remember that weight is mass $\times$ gravitational
field strength (= 10 N/kg on Earth).*

Examination answers and tips

TOPIC 13 – The Solar System

Terminal Paper Questions

1 (a) (i) ~~air resistance~~
~~friction~~
gravity   1

     (ii) ~~smaller than F_B~~
~~the same size as F_B~~
bigger than F_B 1

     (iii) less than the time for
satellite B
~~the same as the time for satellite B~~
~~more than the time for satellite B~~   1

   (b) The satellite takes 1 day to orbit the Earth.
The Earth spins around once in the same time,
so the satellite is always in the same position
above the Earth.   2

Examiner's Tip ✓
*Geostationary satellites all take one day to orbit
the Earth and have to be in orbit above the
equator.*

2   star   1
gravitational   1
elliptical   1
Sun   1

3 (a) 24 hours (1 day)   1

   (b) monitoring satellite   1
lower orbit   1
polar orbit   1
shorter time   1

Examiner's Tip ✓
*Geostationary satellites take one whole day to
orbit the Earth and stay above the same point on
the Earth's surface. Remember that the lower the
orbit the faster the speed of the satellite and the
shorter the time taken for one orbit.*

TOPIC 14 – Stars and the Universe

Terminal Paper Questions

1 (a) water, fossils   2

   (b) (i) search for extra terrestrial intelligence   1

     (ii) a radio telescope   1

Examiner's Tip ✓
*Do not forget the word 'radio'. Just saying
'telescope' will not get the mark.*

     (iii) 10–20 cm (least noise)   1

2 (a) A black hole is the remains of a supernova.   1
It is an area with a very strong gravitational field   1
Nothing can escape from it.   1

Examiner's Tip ✓
*A black hole is black because its gravitational
field is so strong not even light can escape from
it.*

   (b) Black holes are detected because X-rays are
emitted from dust and gases that spiral into
the black hole.   3

3 (a) The Universe started from one point that
exploded, creating space and matter.   2

   (b) (i) Radiation from galaxies is moved towards
the red end of the spectrum   2

     (ii) Red-shift means that galaxies are moving
away. The bigger the red-shift the faster
they are moving. So we think the Universe
is expanding.   3

TOPIC 15 – Waves

Terminal Paper Questions

1

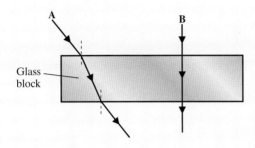

3

Examiner's Tip ✓

Take care with diagrams. Remember to draw in the normals.
Light going into glass refracts towards the normal.
Light going out of glass refracts away from the normal.

2 (a) (i) the wavelength is A   1

       (ii) the amplitude is B   1

  (b) light waves are transverse waves, sound waves are longitudinal waves   1

      light waves can travel through a vacuum, sound waves cannot   1

3 (a)

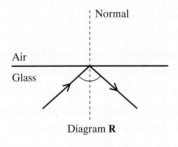

Diagram **R**

1

  (b) (i) total internal reflection   1

Examiner's Tip ✓

You need all three words to get the mark.
Remember TIR can only take place if light is travelling from a more dense to a less dense medium, e.g. glass into air.

      (ii) more information can be carried   1

           there is less weakening of the signal   1

TOPIC 16 – The electromagnetic spectrum

Terminal Paper Questions

1 (a) sterilise medical equipment   1

       ultra violet   1

       television remote controls   1

       microwaves   1

  (b) frequency   1

2 (a) infra red

  (b) microwave

  (c) gamma-rays

  (d) radio waves

Examiner's Tip ✓

Learn the order of the parts of the electromagnetic spectrum and their uses.

3 (a) M   1

  (b) digital signals are less prone to interference and can carry more information in a given cable   1

              1

4 (a) 1. Gamma   1

       2. X-rays   1

  (b) they are able to penetrate human tissue their energy may be absorbed by cells this can kill or mutate the cells   3

Examination answers and tips

TOPIC 17 – Radioactivity

Terminal Paper Questions

1 (a) (i) background   1

       (ii) % from space = 100%
            − (50 + 14 + 11 + 15)%   1
            = 100% − 90% = 10%   1

   (b) (i) alpha   1

       (ii) beta   1

       (iii) gamma   1

   (c) (i) photographic film   1

       (ii) large doses of radiation can burn skin, cause sickness, kill cells, mutate cells (cause cancer)   3

Examiner's Tip ✓
Answer the question in general terms. The exact effect of radiation on the body depends on the type of radiation, the size of the dose, the tissue irradiated and how the radiation enters the body.

TOPIC 18 – Atomic structure, radioactive decay

Terminal Paper Questions

1 (a) (i) electrons   1

       (ii) negatively charged   1

   (b) (i) the alpha particle and the nucleus both have a positive charge, and like charges repel   2

       (ii) some...Y
           nucleus is positively charged
          some rebound... Z
           ...nucleus has large mass
          very few... Z
           ...nucleus is very small   2

Examiner's Tip ✓
Be clear about what the alpha particle scattering experiment shows us about the structure of the atom.

TOPIC 19 – Sound

Terminal Paper Questions

1 (a) (i) A   1

       (ii) D   1

   (b) The pitch of the note would be higher.   1

   (c) The note would be louder.   1

Examiner's Tip ✓
The frequency of a sound gives its pitch. The amplitude of a sound gives its volume.

2 The electronic oscillator creates very high frequency (ultrasound) waves. The vibrations are able to dislodge dirt without taking the watch apart.   2

TOPIC 20 – The Earth

Terminal Paper Questions

1 (a) lithosphere   1
      crust   1
      mantle   1
      tectonic   1

   (b) Earthquakes are most likely to occur at point D Because it is at the boundary between tectonic plates   2

   (c) It is easy to predict when earthquakes will occur.   1

Examiner's Tip ✓
Be careful. The question asks which statement is incorrect.

2 (a) P waves are longitudinal, S waves are transverse   1
      P waves travel faster than S waves   1
      P waves can travel through solids and liquids, S waves can only travel through solids   1

   (b) (i) They are refracted   1

       (ii) The P waves refract, so X and Y have different densities
          S waves cannot travel through liquid, so X is a solid and Y is a liquid.   3

Examination answers and tips

TOPIC 21 – Electronic control circuits

Module Test Questions

1   1 – AND gate

  2 – capacitor

  3 – relay

  4 – LED

2   1 – temperature sensor

  2 – light sensor

  3 – AND sensor

  4 – motor

3   1 – P

  2 – L

  3 – N

  4 – M

Terminal Paper Questions

1 (a) (i) ON

  ON

  ON   1

  (ii) OR gate   1

 (b) (i) NOT gate   1

  (ii) thermistor   1

  (iii) LDR   1

 (c) Heater is on when it is dark and cold   1

  in these conditions the output from the OR gate

  would be 0   1

  the NOT gate changes the 0 to 1   1

Examiner's Tip ✓

*Work logically through the control circuit to work
out what happens. Remember the truth table for
each type of logic gate.*

TOPIC 22 – Moments, momentum, circular motion

Terminal Paper Questions

1 (a) C   1

  The velocity is the same for all vehicles

  C has the greatest mass   1

 (b) F   1

  The mass is the same for all vehicles

  F has the greatest velocity   1

 (c) momentum = mass × velocity   1

  = 1250 kg × 40 m/s   1

  = 50 000 kgm/s   2

Examiner's Tip ✓

*Remember that you must include the unit to get
the final mark.*

2 (a) (i) moment, force, distance   1

  (ii) moment = 30 N × 90 cm = 2700 Ncm   1

Examiner's Tip ✓

*The unit of the final answer is given as newton
centimetres, so leave the distance here in
centimetres when you do the calculation.*

 (b) The force needed will be larger than 30 N as the
  distance from the pivot is less than 90 cm   2

TOPIC 23 – Lenses

Module Test Questions

1 P and S

2 1 – less

2 – longer

3 – more

4 – shorter

3 1 – parallel

2 – real

3 – sharp

4 – focal

Examiner's Tip ✓

Rays of light from distant objects are parallel.

Terminal Paper Questions

1 (a) (i) C   **1**

     (ii) E   **1**

(b)

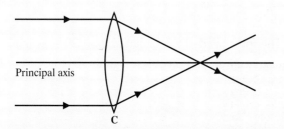

3

Published in 2005 by:
Nelson Thornes Ltd
Delta Place
27 Bath Road
CHELTENHAM
GL53 7TH
United Kingdom

05 06 07 08 09 / 10 9 8 7 6 5 4 3 2 1

A catalogue record for this book is available from the British Library

ISBN 0 7487 9583 9

Page make-up by Tech-Set
Printed in Croatia by Zrinski

Acknowledgements

We would like to thank examiner Pauline Anning for her help with the examination questions, answers and tips.

AQA acknowledgements

AQA examination questions are reproduced by permission of the Assessment and Qualifications Alliance.

Chap. 1 Module 9 – Higher Tier – W 02, Q3; Module 9 – Higher Tier – S 02, Q2; Module 9 – Higher Tier – W 02, Q2; Physics – Foundation Tier 2004, Q7; Chap. 2 Module 9 – Foundation Tier – W 02, Q1; Module 9 – Higher Tier – W 02 Q6.1; Module 9 – Higher Tier – W 02, Q6.2; Chap. 3 Module 9– Foundation Tier S 02, Q1; Module 9– Higher Tier W 02, Q6.3; Module 9– Higher Tier W 02, Q6.4: Physics (Modular) Specification A – Foundation Tier June 2003, Q8; Chap. 4 Module 9– Foundation Tier W 02, Q3; Module 9– Foundation Tier W 02, Q3; Module 9– Foundation Tier S 02, Q7; Science: Double Award (Modular) Foundation Tier - Paper 2 2003, Q13a; Chap. 5 Module 10 – Foundation Tier W 02, Q1; Module 10– Foundation Tier W 02, Q4; Module 10– Foundation Tier S 02, Q6; Physics, Higher Tier, 2004, Q15; Chap. 6 Module 10 Foundation Tier S 02, Q9; Physics – Higher Tier 2004, Q8; Q16; Chap. 7 Module 10 Foundation Tier W 02, Q5; Module 10 Higher Tier S 03, Q4; Chap. 8 Module 10 S 02 – Foundation Tier, Q6; Module 10 W 02 – Foundation Tier, Q2; Module 10 W 02 – Foundation Tier, Q8; Chap. 9 Module 10 S 03 – Higher Tier, Q6; Science: Single Award (Modular) – Higher Tier June 2003, Q10; Chap. 10 Physics (Modular) Specification A – Foundation Tier June 2003, Q2; Physics (Modular) Specification A – Higher Tier June 2003, Q8; Chap. 11 Sci: Paper 2, D.A, Q8; Physics 2004 – Foundation Tier 2004, Q1; Physics 2004 - Higher Tier 2004, Q9; Chap. 12 Physics (Modular) Specification A – Higher Tier June 2003, Q1; Chap. 13 Physics 2004 – Foundation Tier 2004, Q2; Chap. 14 Physics 2004 – Higher Tier 2004 Q2; Physics 2004 – Higher Tier 2004, Q10; Physics (Modular) Specification A – Higher Tier June 2003, Q9; Chap. 15 Science Paper 1 – Foundation Tier 2003, Q8; Physics (Modular) Specification A – Foundation Tier June 2003, Q12; Physics – Higher Tier 2004, Q3; Chap. 16 Physics (Modular) Specification A – Foundation Tier June 2003, Q4; Physics – Higher Tier 2004 Q3 (c); Sci: Paper 1 2003, Q7;Chap. 17 Physics (Modular) Specification A – Foundation Tier June 2003, Q5; Chap. 18 Physics – Foundation Tier 2003, Q11;Chap. 19 Science Double Award – Foundation Tier 2003, Q9; Science: Single Award (Modular) – Higher Tier June 2003, Q8; Chap. 20 Physics – Foundation Tier 2004, Q6; Physics (Modular) Specification A – Higher Tier 2003, Q10; Chap. 21 S03 Module 23, Q1; S02 Module 23, Q2; W02 Module 23, Q2; Physics (Modular) Specification A – Higher Tier June 2003, Q6; Chap. 22 Physics – Higher Tier 2004, Q4; Physics – Higher Tier 2004, Q5; Chap. 23 Foundation Tier – S03, Q6; Foundation Tier – S02, Q4; Foundation Tier – S02, Q3; Foundation Tier – S03, Q6; Foundation Tier – S02, Q4; Foundation Tier – S02, Q3; Physics (Modular) Specification A – Higher Tier June 2003, Q8

AQA take no responsibility for answers given to their questions within this publication.

Photograph acknowledgements

Corel 62 (NT), p.48; Corel 677 (NT), p.9; Corel 681 (NT), p.21; Digital Vision 9 (NT), p.60 (2 photographs); Digital Vision 12 (NT), p.57; Photodisc 31 (NT), p.9; Photodisc 34 (NT), p.65; Photodisc 40 (NT), p.87; Photodisc 54 (NT), p.20; Stuart Sweatmore, p.12.